SEEK FIRST
the KINGDOM

SEEK FIRST
the KINGDOM

Challenging the Culture by Living Our Catholic Faith

by CARDINAL DONALD WUERL

Our Sunday Visitor Publishing Division
Our Sunday Visitor, Inc.
Huntington, IN 46750

Our Sunday Visitor Publishing Division
Our Sunday Visitor, Inc.
200 Noll Plaza
Huntington, IN 46750

ISBN: 978-1-61278-505-9 (Inventory No. T1209)
eISBN: 978-1-61278-206-5
LCCN: 2011940665

Cover design by Lindsey Riesen
Cover art: Shutterstock
Interior design by Sherri L. Hoffman

PRINTED IN THE UNITED STATES OF AMERICA

Table of Contents

Foreword

Mary Ann Glendon

In 2006, the Pontifical Academy of Social Sciences invited six university students, from six different regions of the world, to observe and participate in a conference devoted to the situation of children and young people in today's societies. When the time came for the students to speak, they presented the academicians with some tough questions: What can one person do to help create a more just and peaceful world? How, exactly, does one bring the rich resources of Catholic social thought to bear on the burning issues of our times? One young woman said she often felt overwhelmed by the magnitude of the challenges ahead. She confessed that, "When I look at the daunting problems of the destruction of marriage, abortion, poverty, hunger, child soldiers — I am tempted to feel powerless." But then, wise beyond her years, she told us how she dealt with that feeling. She said, "I know I need to grasp my faith and to begin by living it in the smallest ways, closest to me — in my studies, my work, my future family."

Cardinal Donald Wuerl must have had in mind the countless persons who feel similarly overwhelmed when he took up his pen to write this lucid and encouraging guide to living a Christian vocation amidst the complexities of today's world. Like the young woman at the Roman conference, he begins with the insight that "seeking the kingdom" begins at home — in the sense that we have to change ourselves before we can change the world.

That insight is not a trivial one. For if only one person truly lives his faith in his daily surroundings, that little part of the world is already reclaimed for Christ. And if many people do so — as has happened before in history and could happen again — an entire culture can change and be renewed. As Pope Benedict once put it to a group of young people in St. Peter's Square, "We must have the courage to create islands, oases, and then great stretches of land of Catholic culture where the Creator's design is lived out."

Although seeking the kingdom requires personal conversion, a principal message of this engaging book is that personal transformation is only a beginning. Catholics do not have the option to withdraw into a completely private spirituality. Not even our cloistered contemplatives are exempt from the duty to be salt, leaven, and light in the world in their own distinctive way. The philosopher and martyr Edith Stein, now St. Teresa Benedicta of the Cross, explained this in one of her letters:

> Immediately before, and for a good while after my conversion, I was of the opinion that to lead a religious life meant one had to give up all that was secular and to live totally immersed in thoughts of the divine. But gradually I realized that something else is asked of us in this world and that, even in the contemplative life one may not sever the connection with the world. I even believe that the deeper one is drawn into God, the more one must "go out of oneself"; that is, one must go to the world in order to carry the divine life into it.

For most laymen and laywomen the problem is not severing their connection with the world, but rather that we tend to sever the connections between our faith and the rest of our lives. In contemporary societies where family life, work, worship, recreation, education, and civic activities take place in separate spheres, it is all too easy to relegate religion to a few hours a week spent in prayer or at Mass. From there, it is all too easy to fall into a mindset like that of a professor who once told me, "I happen to be a Catholic, but that has nothing to do with my professional life."

Cardinal Wuerl's book is a forceful rebuttal of the idea that a Christian can keep his faith shut up in a compartment. All Christians, he reminds us, are called not only to "seek" the kingdom, but to "build up" the kingdom. The great dignity of the lay vocation, he writes, is "to take the faith out into the world and give witness everywhere. Lay Catholics go to all the places I, as a bishop, cannot reach. Catholic laymen and laywomen may be standing near the office water cooler when the conversation turns to abortion, or the death penalty, or euthanasia, or immigration. If they know the social teachings of the Church, they are well prepared for the conversation. They are well prepared for *witness*."

Moreover, as the Fathers of the Second Vatican Council emphasized in *Lumen Gentium*, the obligation to work toward the transformation of the world has a definite political dimension: Every Christian in keeping with his or her abilities "has a right and duty to participate in public life, albeit in a diversity and complementarity of forms, levels, tasks and responsibilities." Indeed, "The effort to infuse a Christian spirit into the mentality, customs, laws, and structures of the community in which one lives, is so much the duty and responsibility of the laity that it can never be performed properly by others." Like his predecessor Blessed John Paul II, Pope Benedict XVI has lifted up that message on several occasions, calling for "a new generation of committed lay Christians" capable of "working competently and with moral rigor" in the fields of work, the economy, and politics.

Noting a certain amount of confusion among Catholics on the respective roles of clergy and laity when it comes to public affairs, Cardinal Wuerl reminds us that while bishops and priests have the duty to enunciate and proclaim the principles of Catholic social teaching, it is up to the laity to take those principles and apply them in the public square. He observes ruefully that in his twenty-five years as a bishop he has been told by many political leaders that they hear less often from the Catholic laity than from bishops and priests. If that is so, he wonders, "What is it that keeps people silent?"

Given the richness of Catholic social thought, the reason cannot be lack of material. To be sure, the Church's social teachings do not, and are not intended to, prescribe specific programs and policies. But they do provide a vision and a set of criteria so that those who share in the task of building a good society will have the tools to fashion policies and programs that will serve the common good.

Even the finest set of tools, however, is useless if it remains in the toolbox, or if there is no one with the knowledge to use them. Thus, the Cardinal gently but firmly insists on the responsibility of the laity to acquire a solid foundation in the faith, including the social teachings: "We can't give away anything if we don't first own it ourselves."

How right he is! If our religious education falls short of the general level of secular education, we have trouble defending our beliefs even to ourselves, let alone defending them in public settings. Yet how many of us have put as much effort into deepening our faith formation as we have in keeping up with the latest in information technology? Today's Catholics have had the inestimable good fortune to live in great teaching pontificates. We are members of a Church that possesses a long and distinguished intellectual tradition. Yet it is not without reason that Blessed John Paul II once described Catholic social doctrine as the best-kept secret of the Church.

A solid grounding in the faith, moreover, is only a first step toward effective Christian witness in a pluralistic society. That is why Cardinal Wuerl takes pains to point out that how we say things is as important as what we say:

> As ambassadors of God's kingdom, we need — with every word and gesture — to live out our commitment. We need to be a people of profound respect for the truth. Yes, we have a right to express our thoughts, opinions, and positions. Indeed, we who follow Christ are *duty-bound* to speak the truth, but always with charity, always "in love" (Eph 4:15). It is not enough that we know or believe something to be true. We must express that truth with kindness and with true concern for others, so that the bonds between us can be strengthened in building up the Body of Christ.

That wise advice is particularly timely at a moment when religious freedom in the United States is increasingly menaced by aggressive secularism, the erosion of conscience protection for religious individuals and institutions, threats to the autonomy of religious institutions, and inroads into the rights of parents regarding the education of their children. Now, more than ever, informed Catholics must make their voices heard. One can only say "Amen" to Cardinal Wuerl's plea:

> The voice of Catholic physicians needs to be heard, loud and clear, in the area of health care. Catholic lawyers need to speak out on the administration of justice and our constitutionally protected liberties. Catholic parents and teachers should be involved in educational

issues. Catholic universities and colleges should be in the forefront articulating Catholic principles and providing the intellectual and academic support that allows people to give an account of their faith.

Cardinal Wuerl does not pretend that the Christian witness he calls for will be easy. In our secular society, there is no pat formula for how one can be effective in advancing religiously grounded moral viewpoints in the public square. There are no precise directions for steering between the danger, on the one hand, of being marginalized if one forcefully asserts one's religious convictions, or the opposite danger of being co-opted by the culture as one strives to get into a position where one's views will be taken seriously. Thus one of the many virtues of this book is its abundant use of stories and anecdotes to illustrate each major point.

Recognizing that there will be times when witnessing requires great courage and sacrifice, the author follows John Paul II in urging Catholics to be who they are and to "Be not afraid." He tells us that we must not remain silent: "We must stand up when the kingdom, the Church, the faith, the truth, is attacked, belittled, misrepresented, or ignored. Individually and collectively, quietly or insistently, Christians are called to stand for Christ and his kingdom."

At the heart of this highly accessible book is the fervent belief that the voice and engagement of the laity can play a decisive role in transforming our society, and building the kingdom of peace and justice on earth. Anyone who is inspired to respond to the author's exhortations will find much guidance and encouragement in the chapters that follow.

Mary Ann Glendon
President, Pontifical Academy of Social Sciences

CHAPTER 1

We Look for a Kingdom

Some years ago I served on a committee to evaluate the way biblical texts were used in the liturgy. Around the table sat theologians, biblical scholars, linguists, professors of literature, historians, and bishops. Our work was complex and occasionally challenging. When rendering the Bible for the Church's prayer, clarity is helpful and elegance is elevating, but familiarity is also important. The most common prayers sometimes presented us with surprising difficulty. No task was so vexing as our analysis of the Lord's Prayer, the "Our Father."

I vividly remember the moment when we turned our attention to the line "Thy kingdom come."

"Here is an example of the difficulties we face," said one participant. "People don't know the word 'thy.' They don't speak that way any longer, and that renders the petition unintelligible." Everyone knew where the discussion would go from here: clarity versus familiarity. Do we keep the old-fashioned "thy," because everybody has already learned the prayer that way, or do we change to "your," because everyone talks that way?

But another scholar spoke up: "The problem's not with 'thy,' but with the word 'kingdom.' Most people have little familiarity with what the word means, and few today have any understanding of what Scripture means when it speaks of the kingdom of God." He pointed out that it is the spiritual and theological meaning behind the word that is not understood. However, he went on to note, that is precisely a word that we cannot change lest we lose the opportunity to explain its meaning.

His observation caused all of us to reflect once again on the dual meaning of so many words in Scripture and in the liturgy.

We were, all of us in that room, citizens of a country that traces its founding to the overthrow of a king. For at least a century after the American Revolution, kings and queens were often cast as villains in civic discourse. In countries outside the United States, the monarchs who survived the age of revolutions were reduced to ceremonial roles, appearing in world news briefly, now and then, at the time of a royal wedding.

What Americans know of kingdoms we have learned mostly from history books and fairy tales — unless we've read our Bible carefully or paid attention at Mass.

At Mass each week millions of Catholics profess belief in a kingdom that "will have no end." We pray that "our departed brothers and sisters" may gain "admittance to [God's] kingdom." We ask that we ourselves may "enter into" that kingdom as our "inheritance." We acknowledge that "the kingdom, the power, and the glory are" God's alone. Yet we speak to the Almighty of our own "blessed hope of your kingdom" and "the eternal joy of your kingdom." In hymns we urge one another to "seek first the kingdom of God." And, of course, we pray, "thy kingdom come!"

We dedicate a mystery of the Rosary to "The Proclamation of the Kingdom," and we end our liturgical year with the Feast of Christ the King.

In the New Testament, we find the kingdom everywhere. To Jesus, it seems to be a preoccupation. From the moment he "began to preach," he announced that "the kingdom of heaven is at hand" (Mt 4:17). Jesus spoke of the kingdom's subjects, its power, its boundaries, its duration. Indeed, it was his talk of the kingdom that frightened Pontius Pilate into sentencing him to death (see, for example, Jn 18:33, 37, 39, and 19:19).

All but one of the authors to whom we traditionally ascribe the New Testament books — Matthew, Mark, Luke, John, Peter, James, and Paul — make mention of the kingdom. The only one who does not is Jude, and his letter is so short that he hardly has the time.

Obviously the kingdom should be a matter of some importance to Christians. We make a great deal of it when we pray. So did Jesus, who taught us to pray, "thy kingdom come."

In the course of this book we will consider the kingdom in some detail. We'll look at Jesus' sayings, the apostles' doctrine, and the tradition of the Church. What we'll see is that Jesus was not simply speaking symbolically when he announced the kingdom. This was not just a preferred metaphor. He was urgent and specific about what the kingdom was and what it wasn't, who was in it and who was outside it, and about how one could get in it and stay in it. His kingdom had distinguishing characteristics.

If he had been speaking metaphorically, it would have been an ill-chosen metaphor, since it brought suspicion and persecution upon him, his apostles, and many followers down through the ages. The Romans did not fear a metaphor. Nor did the Persians. Nor have any of their successors in the business of the persecution of Christians. These earthly powers killed Christians because they knew the Christians were serious about a certain king and his kingdom, and they considered that kingdom a threat to their own. God's kingdom was serious business.

It still is. Indeed, in our own day the kingdom is often mis-understood and misconstrued, even by Christians. Some *do* try to dismiss it as a metaphor — a symbol of what the world would be like if more people would be nice to one another. People should be nice to one another; but the kingdom of God is not reducible to niceness. Others bring it up when they want to suggest that Christians are secretly disloyal to the current regime — that the Christian "kingdom" is somehow a code word for theocracy.

In every election year, it seems, we find the kingdom suf-fering violence and taken away, far away, from its original intention. Political parties and candidates like to claim, or strongly suggest, that their agenda is the valid way to apply the Gospel in the world. When they do, secularists will then step forth to argue that religious people have no right whatsoever to "impose" their beliefs by speaking up in public.

We should be prepared for this; and as Christians we should be prepared to give an answer to both errors, to make the necessary distinctions, and to call people to account for their use and misuse of the kingdom of God.

I recall a time when I was visiting dear friends, a young couple with three young and very active boys. The mom sent her husband out on an errand with the children, and I tagged along. As Dad and I sat up front, the three boys played com-petitively in the back and taunted one another. This would go on for a bit till the youngest got frustrated and pushed one or the other offending brother. Each time the dad would say, "Use your words, not your hands," and things would quiet down. But as the game continued, the little child would soon lose his temper again and give another push. After several rep-etitions of "Use your words, not your hands," the youngest boy, in frustration, replied: "I don't have those words!"

We, too, can feel frustrated when we don't have words to respond to the things people say about our Catholic faith.

Many Catholics "don't have those words," either because they've neglected to study the teaching of Christ, or because they haven't had the opportunity.

I would like this book to be an opportunity — at least a beginning — for many people. I would like its readers to finish the last page and "have those words" that will enable them to speak the truth when they find error. I would like many Catholics to "have those words" they need to defend the most vulnerable members of our society. I would like many non-Catholics to "have those words" to speak up for their Catholic friends when those friends are wronged.

If we are Catholics, we want to work for the kingdom. God made us to want it, even if we don't know how to put those desires into words. We want to bring about the kingdom. We mean it when we pray "thy kingdom come." But as adults we need to make an effort to *know what we mean* by such strange words.

A kingdom is recognizable by certain characteristics. It is ruled by a king. Its citizens, the king's subjects, recognize him as their ruler. Its citizens observe the laws and keep the customs of the kingdom. The realm has boundaries, borders, that define the extent of the king's authority.

To speak of a kingdom may feel odd, at first, to an American. But it is the very essence — the *supernatural* message and substance — of the Gospel of Jesus Christ. If we don't "get" the kingdom, we're not getting the Gospel.

We who are both Christian and American may often feel we're living in exceptionally difficult times, that the misunderstanding and even bigotry of many of our contemporaries is somehow unique in history. But it's not. The kingdom is marked, in every age, by signs of contradiction.

Whenever we're tempted to think we're so different, we should consider the words of St. Justin Martyr, set down around the year 155, when the ink of the Gospel was hardly dry on the parchment:

> And when you hear that we look for a kingdom, you suppose, without asking, that we speak of a human kingdom. Instead, we speak of something that is with God, as can be shown from the confession of faith made by those who are charged with being Christians — even though they know that death is the punishment awarded to those who so confess. For if we looked for a human kingdom, we would deny our Christ, so that we might not be killed. We would try to escape detection, so that we might get what we hope for. But since our thoughts are not fixed on the present, we are not concerned when men cut us off; since death is a debt which must at all events be paid.[1]

CHAPTER 2

The Kingdom Is Like . . .

I was speaking to a large group of teens in the Archdiocese of Washington. After I had spoken a little bit, I asked if they had questions. A young woman stood up and asked, "What does the Church have for me?"

On paper the question can seem self-centered or even arrogant. But I wish you could have heard her speak it. Her tone was genuine, seeking, searching, imploring. She was asking because she hoped to get an answer. Somewhere, surely, she had heard or read the promise, "Ask, and you shall receive . . . Seek . . . Knock."

I believe that young woman was doing something Christians have always done. She was *looking for the kingdom*, and she was looking to the Church.

———

There can be no doubt that Christianity is all about "the kingdom." Pope Benedict XVI, as he looks to the kingdom, invokes the words of Jesus, and he even undertakes a numerical analysis of the Word of the Lord. His conclusion is simple and profound.

The core content of the Gospel is this: The kingdom
of God is at hand . . . A look at the statistics underscores
this. The phrase "Kingdom of God" occurs 122 times in
the New Testament as a whole; 99 of these passages are
found in the three Synoptic Gospels [Matthew, Mark,
and Luke], and 90 of these 99 texts report words of Jesus.[2]

The heart of the Gospel is the kingdom. If we want to live
a Christian life — if we want to make a credible claim that we
are followers of Jesus — it's essential that we look to this kingdom he has proclaimed. But where do we look? It's not like
earthly kingdoms, which we can find on a map or a globe. We
can't zoom in on its landscape by using Google Earth. There
are no webcams in the streets of its capital. We cannot collect
its stamps or coins or fly its flag.

This kingdom is real and substantial. It is identifiable. We
can know what it is, and what it's not. And yet it is mysterious. It
is, in fact, a *mystery*. Jesus himself said so, even as he assured his
first disciples that the mystery will be disclosed to them. "The
mystery of the kingdom of God has been granted to you" (Mk
4:11). With eyes of faith we, his latter-day disciples, can "see" and
recognize the kingdom of God, if we look for it in the right places.

———

What is a mystery? And why should we apply that word to
something as huge as the kingdom?

Today we use the word as a synonym for words like
"enigma" and "riddle." We also use it to describe a kind of literature and movies. And there is indeed some common ground
here. A religious mystery can appear enigmatic, and it does
present a challenge to our intellect, just as riddles and Agatha
Christie novels do.

A religious mystery, however, is so much more. It is mysterious and imperceptible to the senses because it is *spiritual*.

Here we come to another word that is often misunderstood. When we speak of "spiritual" things, we often mean something wispy and indefinite, a matter of individual opinion, momentary emotion, and personal preference. We like to say "seeing is believing" and "what you see is what you get," and so we have an innate tendency to treat spiritual matters differently from the way we treat scientific hypotheses or news reports. To many Americans, something spiritual is somehow less true or less real than something material and concrete. Americans like to measure things; and since spiritual realities cannot be measured by the conventional means, we have subjected them to opinion polls, and thus reduced substantial beliefs to mere "values," which can rise and fall based on market activity.

For Christians, however, mysteries are realities so great as to be beyond the capacity of our limited intellect and senses. God made us with these limitations and, in revealing the mysteries, accommodated the message to our capacities. Parents do this all the time with their children. High-school calculus and physics teachers do it every day with their students. Like every good teacher and every loving parent, God has revealed the mysteries of the kingdom by way of analogies, allegories, metaphors — the little stories we Christians refer to as "parables."

Again, it's not that the *kingdom* is a metaphor. The kingdom itself is not a metaphor. It's something supremely real. But Jesus explains the kingdom, which is invisible and spiritual, by comparing it to ordinary, everyday things we know from the world where we live.

———

As Pope Benedict clearly demonstrated, Jesus loved to talk about the kingdom. The Lord proclaimed the kingdom, preached the kingdom, promised the kingdom. But when he wanted to explain it, he couldn't just spell it out the way he might explain the techniques of carpentry or the route from Nazareth to Jerusalem.

Why not?

Well, it will help if we first ask the most basic question: What is the kingdom? How do we define it?

The most basic definition is this: the kingdom of God is the presence of God.

God rules wherever he is present, and he is present everywhere in creation. God created everything, and he holds everything in existence from one moment to the next. "All things came to be through him, and without him nothing came to be" (Jn 1:3). No subatomic particle is so small as to escape God's notice and dominion. No galaxy is so vast as to exceed his powers of governance. God is present in our inner life as well and knows our thoughts better than we know them ourselves.

God is everywhere. Yet we do not experience the divine presence the way we experience material things and events. It's not something we can see with our bodily eyes, or hear with our ears, or touch with our hands. We can't pull our friends aside and say, "Look — over there — there's the kingdom. Do you see it? Don't you see God's presence?"

God is present everywhere, but as a pure spirit he transcends everything in time and space. He dwells *in fullness* in unapproachable light, in heaven. There he is seen, and glorified, by all the angels and saints.

On earth the kingdom is hidden mysteriously and may be encountered anywhere, but only in a spiritual way. We won't find exit signs for it on the interstate. But there are indeed "signs" of the kingdom. To discern them, we need to grow in the ways of prayer. We need to become as keen in our spiritual senses as athletes and musicians are in the use of their physical senses. We need to train our hearts and minds in a disciplined way.

Jesus will deny no one the grace of such growth. In the

Gospels we can follow the same curriculum he used in teaching his closest friends, the twelve apostles. He began their training (and ours) with the so-called "kingdom parables."

———

The word *parable* comes from a Greek word that means comparison. Since we are not equipped to grasp the fullness of the kingdom, Jesus does not present us with the fullness. He compares it to something we already know. He does not say what the kingdom is. He says what it is like.

He says the kingdom is like a valuable pearl (Mt 13:45-46) or a field where a treasure is hidden (Mt 13:44).

He says the kingdom is like seed growing in the ground (Lk 8:5-15) or yeast causing dough to rise (Mt 13:33).

He says the kingdom is like a field of grain that has been maliciously sown with weeds (Mt 13:24-30).

He says the kingdom is like a fishing net that takes in a large catch, but also a measure of trash (Mt 13:47).

What do we learn about the kingdom from these parables?

We learn that the kingdom is something of great value, something for which we should work hard, save our resources, and live lives of self-denial. If we want to accumulate enough money to buy the expensive pearl, or the field where the treasure is hidden, we'll have to forgo many other pleasures along the way. But the story's not about money, really. It's about desire. Do we want the kingdom as intensely as a miser wants treasure? Are we willing to make the kingdom our great priority in life, the goal we're striving for, the purpose of our daily labors?

We learn from Jesus that the kingdom works powerfully, but quietly, gradually, and invisibly, like seed and like yeast. We can't see the growth from one moment to the next, and we can't see how it's happening, but we trust that the process is at work. It is far more than meets the eye.

We learn that Jesus wants his kingdom to include as many people as possible, and so he casts a wide net and he lets it fall to drag the bottom of the lake. If we are willing, he will catch us into his kingdom.

We learn, too, that till the end of the world the kingdom's boundaries will be invisible to us, and on earth God's friends will live and work beside those who live in enmity against the kingdom. There is no uniform or badge, no distinctive cap or cape, that distinguishes saints from sinners. The field grows weeds and wheat, side by side. The net catches fish and trash, all mixed together.

Finally, we learn what we must *do* for the sake of the kingdom. Ours is not merely a passive role. The sower sows his seed, and the seed is the word of God. Our lives are the ground where that seed is scattered, and we're responsible for the condition of that ground. If we are preparing the "soil" by our prayer and good deeds — if we are clearing away the stones and thorns of sin and worldly anxiety — then the kingdom will grow abundantly within us.

Abundantly, but still invisibly.

Jesus used the terms "kingdom of God" and "kingdom of heaven" interchangeably, synonymously. They are terms, as we have seen, that dominate the New Testament. But they are *new* with the New Testament. The phrase "kingdom of God" appears only once, in passing, in the entire Old Testament (Wis 10:10).

Jesus' contemporaries did look for a kingdom, as had their ancestors, but God's plan exceeded all their dreams and desires.

We find the first suggestions of kingship in the Garden of Eden, where Adam was given "dominion over the fish of the sea, the birds of the air, the tame animals, all the wild animals, and all the creatures that crawl on the earth" (Gn 1:26). We know, of course, that Adam's reign ended rather badly. Nevertheless, God's people wished for a king. In time, they begged the Prophet Samuel to "appoint a king over us, like all the nations, to rule us" (1 Sm 8:5). Theirs was not a holy desire. They wanted a king for the sake of earthly power. Samuel urged them to let God alone be their king. But the people insisted, in spite of God's warnings about taxation and forced military service. So Samuel anointed a king for them, and then another king. Eventually, the divine warnings proved true, and once again human kingship ended badly, with a weakened, divided kingdom laid waste by its enemies.

But first there was a king named David, and God promised that through David's house — his line, his seed — a king would come who would rule forever and bring peace and prosperity to the land. That king would be God's anointed. The word for "anointed" is *moshiach* in Hebrew, *christos* in Greek. That king would be the Messiah. He would be the Christ. King David's reign, though imperfect, provided a prototype and a point of reference for future generations of God's people in Israel.

Their hope sustained them as they suffered conquest, exile, dispersion, servitude, humiliation, and oppression. The prophets foretold fulfillment in the grandest terms. The kingdom of the Messiah would be a continual feast, a lavish banquet, a time of healing and justice.

Jesus spoke of his own ministry in just such extravagant terms: "the blind regain their sight, the lame walk, lepers are cleansed, the deaf hear, the dead are raised, the poor have the good news proclaimed to them" (Lk 7:22). He announced his mission very dramatically in another scene in St. Luke's Gospel. There we see Jesus worshipping in his hometown synagogue on the Sabbath, and he turns to a passage in the Prophet Isaiah and reads:

"The Spirit of the Lord is upon me, because he has anointed me to bring glad tidings to the poor. He has sent me to proclaim liberty to captives and recovery of sight to the blind, to let the oppressed go free, and to proclaim a year acceptable to the Lord."

Rolling up the scroll, he handed it back to the attendant and sat down, and the eyes of all in the synagogue looked intently at him.

He said to them, "Today this scripture passage is fulfilled in your hearing" (Lk 4:18-21).

He was inaugurating the kingdom of the Messiah. He was saying, in terms everyone could recognize — terms borrowed from the prophets (see Is 61) — that the kingdom had come. The waiting was over.

Some people recognized him immediately as king, because of the signs he mentioned: miraculous cures and other marvels. They called him "Son of David," which was a royal title. But Jesus' kingship was not apparent to everyone, because many people expected the king to be a warrior, like the mightiest of their long-ago monarchs. It's not that the people wanted worldly power *instead of* righteousness and godliness. They expected both. But Jesus presented them with an unexpected sort of power and a very different notion of kingship.

Thus he began with what they knew, what they longed for, what they looked for: a kingdom. But he spoke to them in parables about what they could not yet know: that the kingdom would be greater than anything they had imagined or could imagine. It would be the very kingdom of heaven come to earth. Its power would be greater than any power possible in the natural world; it would be supernatural, visible only through eyes of faith.

The kingdom of heaven is like that.

CHAPTER 3

The Kingdom and the Church

In his book *Jesus of Nazareth*, Pope Benedict XVI told the story of a skeptical scholar of the nineteenth century, a wayward priest who had lost his faith. The man complained that Jesus had promised the world a kingdom, but all he left us was the Church.

It's not a unique story. Most of us have encountered the same attitude.

Once, back in the early 1980s, I was preparing for confessions at a parish, and I was approached by a man who told me he had left the Church twenty-five years earlier.

I tried to make reentry a little easier for him by striking up a conversation. "What kept you away?" I asked.

"You," he replied.

I was stunned. I had not been a priest for as long as he'd been away. I stumbled a bit as I tried to respond: "I beg your pardon. I don't think I've ever . . . "

"Oh no," he said, "I don't mean you *personally*. I just mean the Church." After he thought out loud a little while longer, he concluded, "I can't believe I gave up something that means so much to me."

That's the difficulty, isn't it? Jesus promised a kingdom, but he gave the world . . . me! And you. And about a billion others who are very much like you and me, with all our faults and failures and human limitations. Who can blame that man for being disappointed with what he saw of the Church?

Jesus promised a kingdom, but he left a Church. What *was* he thinking?

———

We're fortunate to know a bit about what he was thinking, because he told us.

We know, for example, that the kingdom is primarily spiritual and invisible. "Asked by the Pharisees when the kingdom of God would come, [Jesus] said in reply, 'The coming of the kingdom of God cannot be observed, and no one will announce, "Look, here it is," or, "There it is." For behold, the kingdom of God is among you'" (Lk 17:20-21).

That last sentence can be (and has been) translated as "the kingdom of God is *within* you," suggesting an interior reality — something that abides in the heart and mind of the believer.

Thus we know that the kingdom is spiritual, invisible, interior. Yet it is still more than that. You and I are human, and so we are composite creatures. We are composed of a spiritual soul and a material body. Both elements are essential and indispensable to our humanity. In a similar way, the kingdom is interior, but also has an exterior element or dimension. To emphasize the spiritual is not to deny the material.

For the kingdom, as Jesus proclaimed it, abides inwardly, but also makes itself known by evidence — by manifestations. It breaks through.

Consider the scene in the Gospel when Jesus is approached by the disciples of John the Baptist. They ask him: "Are you the one who is to come, or should we look for another?" Jesus said to them in reply, "Go and tell John what you have seen and heard: the blind regain their sight, the lame walk, lepers are cleansed, the deaf hear, the dead are raised, the poor have the good news proclaimed to them" (Lk 7:20-22).

Elsewhere, Jesus commanded his disciples to announce the kingdom — and not just by their words, but also by their wondrous deeds. "As you go, make this proclamation: 'The kingdom of heaven is at hand.' Cure the sick, raise the dead, cleanse lepers, drive out demons" (Mt 10:7-8). Again, the kingdom is invisible, heavenly, and so it must be announced. But it is also manifest by certain signs. When the disciples worked wonders, they were to let people know that physical healing was a sign of a still greater wonder. Jesus said: "Cure the sick . . . and say to them, 'The kingdom of God is at hand for you'" (Lk 10:9).

Throughout the Bible, God's people are set apart by spiritual gifts, but also by certain outward signs. In the Old Testament, these signs were tribal, ethnic, territorial, and legal. Eventually, they flourished in the kingdom of David. In the New Testament, God's people dwell in the kingdom of the Son of David, the kingdom of heaven, the kingdom of God.

In both the Old Testament and the New, the kingdom constitutes a religious society that has been summoned, formed, and founded by God. In both the Old Testament and the New, God endows that society with certain forms and characteristics that make it recognizable.

The kingdom announced by Jesus would be both heavenly and earthly. As he explained it: "All power in heaven and on earth has been given to me" (Mt 28:18). Thus we see that the kingdom — with its power and glory — resides with Jesus. In the following verses, however, we find that Jesus delegated that power to human beings, his apostles, giving them specific instructions: "Go, therefore, and make disciples of all nations, baptizing them in the name of the Father, and of the Son, and of the holy Spirit, teaching them to observe all that I have commanded you. And behold, I am with you always, until the end of the age" (Mt 28:19-20).

In a previous chapter we've noted that the kingdom of God is synonymous with the *presence of God*. Now, we see that Jesus promised that his special presence would accompany a certain religious society — a certain group of disciples — "always," till the end of time.

He chose to identify his kingdom with a clearly recognizable society. You'll know it, for example, by its rituals: baptism and the blessing in the name of the Trinity. You'll know it by its laws: Jesus' commandments and beatitudes, which his people observe. You'll know it by its doctrines: what the apostles teach. What's more, you'll know it because it is universal (the Greek word for universal is *katholikos*, "Catholic"). The kingdom of God includes both heaven and earth, and on earth it extends not just to territorial or ethnic Israel, but to "all nations."

Many of these themes come together in the passage where Jesus appoints Peter to be the leader of the apostles: "And so I say to you, you are Peter, and upon this rock I will build my Church, and the gates of the netherworld shall not prevail against it. I will give you the keys to the kingdom of heaven. Whatever you bind on earth shall be bound in heaven; and whatever you loose on earth shall be loosed in heaven" (Mt 16:18-19).

So we are confronted with some curious facts. Jesus gave Peter "the keys to the kingdom of heaven," but also the authority to "bind on earth." He appointed Peter to govern a "kingdom," but Peter's governance would be the foundation for a "Church." He spoke of the kingdom as something already accomplished and present (see, for example, Mt 3:2), yet also something still to come in the future (see Mt 13:43).

Our Lord promised a kingdom. He gave us the Church. The Scriptures are clear on this point: if we wish to find the kingdom, now or in the future, we must first find the Church.

———

Jesus presents us with genuine mysteries, but the *Catechism of the Catholic Church* helps us to sort them out.

"The kingdom of heaven was inaugurated on earth by Christ," says the *Catechism*, which goes on to explain that the kingdom "shone out" in the word, works, and presence of Jesus. "The Church is the seed and beginning of this kingdom. Its keys are entrusted to Peter."[3]

God's reign "already exists and will be fulfilled at the end of time. The kingdom has come in the person of Christ and grows mysteriously in the hearts of those incorporated into him."[4]

Thus we learn that Christ has established his kingdom on earth, though not in the fullness of its glory. It is here, but it is still growing. "At the end of time, the Kingdom of God will come in its fullness."[5] In the meantime, "Christ the Lord already reigns through the Church."[6] In the Church we encounter his doctrine, his law, his earthly and heavenly authority, and all his sacraments. If Christ said something about his kingdom, you can look for it in his Church. He said, for example, that there would be some disciples who would live celibate lives, renouncing marriage "for the sake of the kingdom" (Mt 19:12), and you can still find those disciples today, in the Catholic Church.

The kingdom is present wherever the king is present, and nowhere is his presence so "real," so *substantial*, as in the Church's liturgy. When we speak of the mystery at the heart of the Mass, we call it the "Real Presence." It's not that the king is absent everywhere else, but he willed that we should encounter him there in a unique and powerful way, as at the time of his Incarnation. In the Eucharist, the king appears in his body, blood, soul, and divinity; and he comes to make his dwelling within and among his faithful people. Moreover, he shares with them his life, including his kingship, as we "come to share in the divine nature" (2 Pt 1:4).

Nowhere does Christ so immediately fulfill our petition "thy kingdom come" as when he comes to us in the Holy Mass. Thus, the *Catechism* says, the "Holy Spirit's transforming power in the liturgy hastens the coming of the kingdom and the consummation of the mystery of salvation."[7]

In sharing his life and his divine nature, Christ also shares his kingship with those who receive him, and they are given power to extend his presence in the world. The kingdom is within them! And so the kingdom grows still more.

———

The Eucharist is the Body and Blood of Christ — a share of God's nature. Yet it tastes as bland as an unsalted cracker, and it is unimpressive to look at.

The Good News comes to us with words inspired by God himself. Yet it comes in a book that's small and written, scholars tell us, in rough Greek.

The kingdom has come with power. Yet it has its beginning in the Church, and it looks a lot like you and me.

That man who discussed confession with me so many years ago left the Church because of the scandal of its humanity, but eventually he figured out that he had also lost "something that means so much" to him: the kingdom.

This is the faith of the Church today, but it was also the faith of the early Christians. Writing in the third century, Origen of Alexandria said: "We are even in the present life placed in the Church, which is the form of the kingdom that is to come."[8] The greatest of the Church Fathers, St. Augustine, discussed it in terms of an almost mathematical equivalency.

In one place he says, "Thus the Church is already now the kingdom of Christ and the kingdom of heaven."[9] Elsewhere he wrote: "The present Church is the kingdom of Christ and the kingdom of God."[10]

It's not that these men lived in a purer time. It's not that they never faced the kind of scandals that make people want to leave the Church. Jesus himself warned that scandals would always be part of life on earth (see Lk 17:1).

Augustine wrote as scathingly of those scandals as anyone else. Yet he had also studied the kingdom parables — just as we do today — and so he knew that the scandalous behavior of a few Christians will not invalidate the Church. Much less will it void the kingdom of God. He pondered the wheat field and the dragnet, but he settled on John the Baptist's image of the threshing floor (Lk 3:17). These are the words of a homily Augustine preached at the end of the fourth century:

> Don't be surprised, either, at how many bad Christians there are, who fill the church, who take communion at the altar, who loudly praise the bishop or the priest when he preaches about good morals . . . They can be with us in the Church of this time; but in that Church which will come into being after the resurrection, they will be unable to be gathered in with the saints.
>
> The Church of this time, you see, is compared to a threshing-floor, having on it grain mixed with chaff, having bad members mixed with good; after the judgment it will have all the good members, without any bad ones. This threshing-floor holds the harvest sown by the apostles, watered by the teachers who followed them up till the present time . . .
>
> If you are good, then, you must put up with the bad; if you are bad, you must imitate the good. The fact is,

on this threshing-floor grains can degenerate into chaff, and again grains can be resurrected from chaff. This sort of thing happens every day, my dear brothers and sisters; this life is full of both painful and pleasant surprises. Every day people who seemed to be good fall away and perish; and again, ones who seemed to be bad are converted and live . . .[11]

We need to be patient with one another — even as we are impatient with the pace of the kingdom's growth.

If we are hurt by scandals, if we can't see the kingdom because it is obscured by the bad behavior of some Christians, we must commit ourselves to still deeper faith.

If we must be impatient, we should express ourselves not by dramatically leaving the kingdom, just as it's beginning in the Church, but by more urgently petitioning the king: *Thy kingdom come!*

CHAPTER 4

Signs of the Kingdom

In children's books and Disney movies, you can always tell when you're approaching the good kingdom. You see high alabaster walls and a skyline of gleaming spires, towers, and turrets. The sky is always blue. The sun is always shining. Banners billow in a gentle breeze. In storybooks these elements are signs of the magical kingdom. Artists in the Middle Ages depicted their earthly kingdoms in a similarly idealized way. Unfortunately, no earthly kingdom lives up to its imaginary signs.

Jesus' kingdom also came with signs. His signs, however, have proven to be most durable. After two millennia, they are still strong and still strengthening God's people. They still manifest the kingdom of heaven throughout the nations of the earth.

In the last chapter we mentioned some of these signs in passing. Here we should dwell on them for a bit.

Indeed, if we read the Gospels closely, we find the evangelists referring to Jesus' miracles as "signs" (see, for example, Jn 2:11). St. John does this so often that scholars call the first half of his Gospel the "Book of Signs."

What are these signs? We mentioned them before: "the blind regain their sight, the lame walk, lepers are cleansed, the deaf hear, the dead are raised."

Why are they *signs?* Because they do what signs do: they point to something else. They are actual historical events — real marvels — but they were intended for a more marvelous purpose.

If you see a sign on the interstate, it's just a piece of metal, but it symbolizes a greater reality: a city or a state, a street or a neighborhood — a destination. A sign always points to something greater than itself. Jesus' signs, awesome as they are, also do this: they point beyond themselves, to a greater truth.

We see this most clearly in the well-known story of Jesus' healing of a paralyzed man (see Mk 2:3-12). The man's friends acted in a kindly and heroic way: they lowered his stretcher through the roof of the place where Jesus was staying. Jesus was so impressed by their faith, shown in this good deed, that he gave the paralyzed man a tremendous gift. He told him: "your sins are forgiven." Well, that statement scandalized some of the onlookers, who thought (rightly) that only God could remit sins.

Jesus, however, *is* God; and so he knew their thoughts, and he asked: "Why are you thinking such things in your hearts? Which is easier, to say to the paralytic, 'Your sins are forgiven,' or to say, 'Rise, pick up your mat, and walk'?"

They did not answer. So Jesus continued: "But that you may know that the Son of Man has authority to forgive sins on earth . . . " and he said to the paralytic, "Rise, pick up your mat, and go home." With the whole crowd looking on, the man did as Jesus had commanded him.

Jesus performed a great miracle. He cured a paralyzed man. But he wanted to make sure everyone understood that the physical cure was not the most important thing. It was a *sign*, intended to point toward something else. It was a sign of Jesus' *"authority . . . on earth"* — a sign of his kingship over all facets of human life, both spiritual well-being and bodily health. The cure was a sign of the kingdom.

It is sad that so many of the onlookers could not discern the true miracle that was happening in front of them. God was present there, and he was forgiving sins, as only God can do.

It is easy for us, too, to misunderstand the meaning of the Gospel story, even though Jesus took great pains to explain himself. We get caught up in the spectacular event, the miraculous healing, and we miss the greater reality that it signifies: the forgiveness of sins. It's as if we see the things we want very badly to see — the grandeur of the castles and the beautiful banners — but we miss what those things urgently signify: the kingdom. In the story of the paralytic, we are witnesses to one great moment when the kingdom broke through, like a brilliant blossom in early spring.

A blossom, though, is passing — here for a moment, then gone for the year. In the city where I live, every year we celebrate the National Cherry Blossom Festival amid lavish natural beauty. The window of opportunity for it is rather narrow, as cherry blossoms usually bloom and fall within a few weeks. Earthly kingdoms, too, have their signs of glory, but these will all fade and fall. If you travel abroad, you can visit their ruins and imagine what they were like in their glory days.

Jesus' kingdom is different from those. His "reign is a reign for all ages" and his "dominion for all generations" (Ps 145:13). The reign of God has outlasted all the dynasties of the earth, and its signs also will endure forever, never falling into ruin.

In the Catholic Church we speak of many signs of God's kingdom, but seven stand apart, and those are the sacraments. We say, according to a classic formula, that the sacraments are efficacious signs of grace, instituted by Christ and entrusted to the Church. The sacraments are *signs* with an important difference: they don't merely *signify*; they also *effect what they signify*. The word "healing" is just the sign or symbol of a cure. Sacraments are like words that actually do the healing. They are signs of God's life — yes, absolutely — but they are signs that do more than teach us about God's life; they give us God's life!

In forty-five years of priesthood and a quarter-century as a bishop, I have written and preached much about the sacraments. I have administered all seven, and more times than I can count. The sacraments are my life, and it is a life I deeply love. Later in the book I've dedicated three chapters to individual discussions of three of the sacraments.

Here, however, I will speak about them only briefly and in passing, as I am primarily interested in them as the divinely established signs of God's kingdom. The seven sacraments are baptism, Eucharist, confirmation, penance (also known as "confession" or "reconciliation"), anointing of the sick, matrimony, and holy orders.

Christ appeared visibly on earth and established here these visible signs of his kingdom — the essential elements of the Church's life. In the sacraments, he gives us things we could not gain through our own efforts. Jesus mentioned forgiveness, and that's true enough. Only God can forgive offenses committed against divine law. But forgiveness is only the beginning. From the abundance of the kingdom's treasury, we receive strength, wisdom, peace, clarity, resolve, endurance, selflessness. We receive it all as grace.

The early Christians applied the lesson of Jesus' healing of the paralytic to their understanding of all the sacraments. They often said: Forgiving a sinner is a greater miracle than raising the dead.

This is something to think about every time we approach the altar for Holy Communion, and every time the priest pronounces the words of absolution at the end of confession. We don't want to be like Jesus' contemporaries and get so caught up in the signs that we miss their significance.

Jesus identified one of these signs as the entryway to the kingdom. He used the most solemn form of speech, a double amen, when he told Nicodemus: "Amen, amen, I say to you, no one can enter the kingdom of God without being born of water and Spirit" (Jn 3:5). Baptism is the only birth "of water and Spirit," and Jesus has explicitly associated it with entry into the kingdom. It is the only way. Elsewhere, he elaborated to his disciples: "Whoever believes and is baptized will be saved; whoever does not believe will be condemned" (Mk 16:16).

These signs of the kingdom are the kingdom's true power. That is as true of the other sacraments as it is of baptism. The sacraments give us what we need to live faithfully on earth as we await the fullness of the kingdom, which will come, for you and me and everyone, at the moment willed by God.

Nevertheless, the sacraments are not the only signs of God's kingdom. They are primarily for the sake of the faithful. They admit us to the kingdom, and they empower us to remain in the kingdom.

Their grace, however, does not terminate in our hearts. We are to bring God's life and love to a world that desperately needs it. We in turn must become like "sacraments" of his presence wherever we may find ourselves.

In the hymns we sing at Mass, we celebrate this fact: "God's blessing sends us forth / strengthened for our task on earth . . . May God with us remain / Through us his Spirit reign."

When we correspond to God's grace, we are extending the kingdom. It is breaking through, shining through, in our deeds wherever we go — at home, at work, at leisure, at school, in the neighborhood, on our sickbed, and even on our deathbed.

This is how Christianity changed the world. The Church had little influence in the corridors of imperial power, but the kingdom broke through in spite of those limitations. It broke through in the lives of the faithful.

One of the great early preachers of the kingdom was a bishop named John. He preached so beautifully that his congregations called him "Golden Mouth," which in Greek is *Chrysostomos*. We know him as St. John Chrysostom. When he preached, he urged his people to take the kingdom home with them after Mass! "Let's show forth a new kind of life. Let's turn earth into heaven! Let's show the Greeks the great blessings they are missing. For, when they see in us good conversation, they will look upon the very face of the kingdom of heaven . . . They will say: 'If the Christians become angels here, what will they be after they leave this world?' Thus they too will be converted."[12]

When we live up to what we have received from God, we become like sacraments ourselves. The more the kingdom breaks through, the more we make our earth into heaven. We ourselves live like angels when we live our sacramental life to the fullest. St. John Chrysostom points out that this is the joy of heaven, and we can anticipate it right now. On another occasion he preached: "Let us love God as we should. This divine and pure love is indeed the kingdom of heaven; this is fruition, this is blessedness . . . For thus we shall see his kingdom even in this life, and shall be living the life of angels, and while we abide on earth we shall be in as goodly a condition as those who dwell in heaven."[13]

Heaven on earth, he promises us. How can that be? Here's how the *Catechism* explains it: "To live in heaven is 'to be with Christ.' The elect live 'in Christ,' but they retain, or rather find, their true identity, their own name. For life is to be with Christ; where Christ is, there is life, *there is the kingdom*."[14]

In order for us to live this way — to manifest the kingdom — we must live an integrated life. We must take the kingdom with us wherever we go. Our lives must be signs of the kingdom, visible to all who stand outside the realm established by Jesus Christ. We cannot isolate certain hours of our day and set them apart from our life in Christ. God is present everywhere, and to be a Christian is to recognize his dominion in every place, at every hour.

To do otherwise is to be a hypocrite. Jesus was patient, kind, and merciful, but hypocrites placed themselves beyond the limits of his forbearance (see Mt 6:2, 5, 16; 15:7; 22:18; 23:13, 15, 23, 25, 27, 29; 24:51, and that's just one Gospel!).

To be in the kingdom is to be with Christ always, and to be *for* Christ always, in season and out of season, in private and in public, on the job and on our days off.

We are the signs of the kingdom, signs that should abide even if everything else should fall to ruin.

CHAPTER 5

The Kingdom in the Public Square

In the last chapter we saw that the Church's sacraments are outward signs of a kingdom that is, at least partially, an inward reality. "The kingdom of God is among you" (Lk 17:21). As spiritual events, the sacraments are profoundly personal and individual. As signs, however, they are unavoidably social: signs, after all, are a means of interpersonal communication.

Yes, the sacraments strengthen us as individuals, but they also strengthen our bonds with others *in Christ*. The sacraments unite us to his body, which is the Church (see, for example, Col 1:18, 24). We are to love whomever Jesus loves. We are to love as Jesus loves. That means we are to love everyone, and love in a self-giving way: For "God our savior . . . wills everyone to be saved and to come to knowledge of the truth. For there is one God. There is also one mediator between God and the human race, Christ Jesus, himself human, who gave himself as ransom for all" (1 Tm 2:3-6).

Salvation — the condition of being saved — is to live in the kingdom. We want everyone to join us as we live in Christ, as we live in his body, the Church. Unlike earthly kingdoms, however, ours will take no one by conquest, no one by coercion. Instead we pray for them. We converse with them. We befriend them. We invite them. We share our faith with them. We persuade them.

Much of our persuasion takes place not through our words, but through our deeds. Our lives themselves are signs of the kingdom. In the small actions of every day, we build up the kingdom in a permanent way — when a mother smiles lovingly at her child, when the child responds to that love with deeds, when a neighbor lends a hand to a neighbor, when a laborer encourages and guides a younger coworker. None of these good works will be lost with time. Each will go on forever, as a sign of the love and faith that comes from Christ and comes through the Church.

Our lives, after all, are expressions of our most profound personal convictions. This is true not only for Christians, of course. Most people, if asked, would say that they try to live their lives according to some important basic principles. The United States of America has become a great nation insofar as it has encouraged its citizens to live up to their beliefs, to communicate their convictions, to apply their principles to public life. Our nation, which boasts of a free-market economy, is better known as a free marketplace of ideas — as the place where many philosophies and religions can coexist in dialogue and prove themselves in service.

Christians have thrived in this environment. In fact, the nation's founding principles would have been inconceivable apart from their grounding in Christian assumptions. Consider the opening claims of the Declaration of Independence: "We hold these truths to be self-evident, that all men are created equal, that they are endowed by their Creator with certain unalienable Rights, that among these are Life, Liberty and the pursuit of Happiness." The founders also appeal to "the laws of nature and of nature's God."

To us today those "truths" may indeed *seem* self-evident, but they are not. The equality of all human beings, the universality of human rights — these principles are still rejected by many governments. It is at least arguable that they are unthinkable apart from a conception of the "Creator" that is our common spiritual heritage. It is at least arguable that human equality is unthinkable apart from a conception of each human being as a "creature" made in the image and likeness of God (see Gn 1:26-27).

As Christians we witness to these principles because we know that they are basic values of God's kingdom. This principled stand has been a tremendous benefit to this country where we spend our earthly lives. We speak against inequity and oppression. We stand for human rights, especially the most fundamental right: the right to life. In other nations, in the last century, Christian men and women have defended these same principles — and have been martyred for their trouble by antireligious regimes (Soviet Russia, Nazi Germany, Republican Spain). The Church continues to add new names to her martyrology. Within the lifetime of many readers of this book, Christians continued to die for the faith in Mexico, Poland, Vietnam, the Middle East, Hungary, as well as in portions of Africa.

In a democracy, principles matter; and in public debate our principles should be at least as welcome as anyone else's. This is the conversation that will lead to law, and no earthly law is neutral. All human laws are based upon certain foundational notions of right and wrong, and these cannot be demonstrated by any empirical means. We arrive at them through our participation in civic life, where all debate proceeds from some kind of religious conviction. Even the most vehement atheist, even the most convinced agnostic, must have recourse to certain truths they believe to be "self-evident" — yet these truths may not be evident to their opponents who believe that rights belong only to the powerful.

Just a few years after Jesus ascended to heaven, St. Paul wrote to the Philippians, who were proud Roman citizens, though they lived in a colony in Greece; and he told them something that probably shocked them. "Our citizenship," he said, "is in heaven" (Phil 3:20). Paul wrote those words to people who were proud of their Roman citizenship, as he himself was (see Acts 22:25). Yet he knew that such earthly ties must be subordinated to a greater allegiance: his ties to the kingdom of heaven.

That is as true for Christians living in twenty-first-century America as it was for Christians living in first-century Roman Philippi. What's more, it's better for the countries where they hold their "secondary" citizenship as well. Roman civilization benefited from the unique contributions of Christians. American history, as we have already seen, has benefited from Judeo-Christian principles since its founding.

———

Recently I participated in a panel discussion at a secular university. A professor asked me point-blank what, if anything, religious people thought they contributed to society.

I answered his question with a question. I asked him what he thought the world would be like — but, more particularly, what he thought our country would be like — if it were not the heir to the millennia of religious instruction and inspiration found in the Ten Commandments, the beatitudes, the golden rule ("Do unto others as you would have them do unto you"), and Jesus' "new commandment" to "love one another."

My inquisitor, to his credit, admitted, "It would be a mess."

Americans take so much Christianity for granted. We assume that our morality is basic equipment that comes standard with human nature. To a certain extent it is. God created all people with a conscience that can discern the natural moral law. But human nature is weakened by original sin, which we've inherited from our first parents, and our conscience is further hindered by our actual sins. (G.K. Chesterton said that the doctrine of original sin — and our subsequent weakness — is the only empirically verifiable Christian doctrine.) God has done us a great favor by giving the law to us in clear terms through divine revelation. The Church has done all of humanity a great favor by preaching this revelation to the whole world.

Few people may care to study ancient history today, but serious students of the past know that pre-Christian paganism could not muster the moral arguments to do away with chattel slavery. Pre-Columbian Aztec Mexico gloried in the blood-drenched altars of human sacrifice. The pre-Christian world did not find compelling reasons to endorse qualities we now consider virtues — like mercy and humility, which were often viewed as signs of weakness. Universal equality and universal rights were not, and could not be, self-evident propositions apart from a background of biblical religion. "Nature's God" knew that we could not reliably arrive at "the laws of nature" without a supernatural visitation. So "nature's God" took flesh in Jesus Christ, who established a kingdom.

We have been given a great gift — in our understanding of the natural law, the revelation of divine law. If we are silent about it — if we do not share that gift with our society — we are as culpable as if we withheld food from neighbors who were starving.

This is a task for which we were created. This is a task for which we were baptized. The Catholic Church teaches that all Christians share in the "apostolate" of Jesus Christ. We all share, to some extent, in the work of an apostle. An apostle, according to the word's root meaning, is someone who is *sent*

— an ambassador — someone sent into the world, to spread the Good News, to make disciples of all nations, to establish the kingdom and build it up with every action of every day.

———

When Christians receive the Sacrament of Baptism, and again when they're confirmed, they are anointed with chrism. We say they are "christened." What does this gesture mean?

In the ancient world, anointing was a ritual that set someone on an exalted vocational path. Priests were anointed for their task. So were prophets. So were kings. For royalty in the ancient world, the religious ceremony of anointing was the equivalent of a modern coronation.

Christians are anointed to share in Christ's threefold office of priest, prophet, and king. In this kingdom we are all "heirs of God and joint heirs with Christ" (Rom 8:17), and so we share in his call to proclaim his law in whatever corner of the kingdom he, in his providence, assigns to us. It may be a home in the suburbs or a desk in a corporate cubicle. It may be a station on an assembly line. It may be an urban apartment. The possibilities are as varied as God's people. All are called to be Christ, wherever they find themselves. All are called to bring about the kingdom.

That's how the kingdom comes. That's how it's manifest in our world, through the love we introduce into the world, the love of Christ. It's his love. It's his Spirit that works through us, by virtue of our baptism. It's his power that will build up the kingdom wherever we go.

Over the past years, as a tribute to those who in so many ways help to realize the kingdom, we designated in this local Church a special award, "Manifesting the Kingdom." People from each of our parishes and many of our organizations were singled out at both the local and archdiocesan levels for recognition for what they do, oftentimes quietly and unheralded, but consistently and persistently, to manifest God's kingdom among us. The most recent celebration, last Epiphany, brought thousands of people to this occasion of joyful salute to those effectively manifesting the kingdom among us.

All of our actions — every kind word we speak, every gesture of generosity — sets in motion a series of future events that will continue forever. If we live this way all our lives, unselfishly, we will know the satisfaction of heaven even now, in a partial way, as we see the kingdom manifest around us.

This is the great dignity of the lay vocation — to take the faith out into the world and give witness everywhere. Lay Catholics go to all the places I, as a bishop, cannot reach. Catholic laymen and laywomen may be standing near the office water cooler when the conversation turns to abortion, or the death penalty, or euthanasia, or immigration. If they know the social teachings of the Church, they are well prepared for the conversation. They are well prepared for *witness*. I have no access to that corner of the workplace. Nor am I privy to the conversations that go on at the sidelines of Little League baseball games, or in the break room at the hospital, or at the counter in the truck stop, or in the chambers of city council. Those are not the places where God has called me. I give thanks, though, because God has called forth Christians to be in all those places.

Every once in a while I'll hear someone say "Why doesn't the Church do more?" They say it about poverty, abortion, medical care, social welfare, and many other issues. "Why doesn't the Church do more to see that Christian values are reflected in our laws, in our culture, in our society?"

A more important question is: Who is the Church?

We all are. The Church is made up of faithful women and men, very few of whom are called to leadership roles as clergy. The clergy are indeed charged with teaching, leading, and sanctifying the laity; but it is the laity who are called to transform the world. Priests strive to make the Church holy. Lay people are to make the world holy. They do it by the witness of their lives.

The clergy, in their preaching and teaching, must make clear the content of God's revelation. But the laity must work to apply that revelation to their walks of life: parenting, law, industry, education, commerce, banking, baking, government, medicine, military, media . . . everything. In doing so, they are exercising their share of the kingship of Christ. Here's how the *Catechism* puts it: "the People of God shares in the royal office of Christ . . . [and] fulfills its royal dignity by a life in keeping with its vocation to serve with Christ."[15] "By reason of their special vocation it belongs to the laity to seek the kingdom of God by engaging in temporal affairs and directing them according to God's will . . . "[16] "As leaven in the dough, the newness of the kingdom should make the earth 'rise' by the Spirit of Christ. This must be shown by the establishment of justice in personal and social, economic and international relations, without ever forgetting that there are no just structures without people who want to be just."[17]

Some people think the Church should use brute strength to change the structures of the world, but that's not our calling. As the *Catechism* tells us, there are no just structures without just people. Just people will change the structures of the world, in a quiet and hidden way, like yeast leavening, like seeds germinating. If enough hearts are changed, people will be changed. If enough people are changed, the world will also be changed.

Why doesn't the Church do more? That's a question all Catholics must ask themselves: *Why don't I do more?*

More than seventy years ago, there was a man named Joseph Stalin, who ruled as a king (though he never held the title) over a vast earthly kingdom (though he called it a "union"). Once, a diplomat asked Stalin what he would do to win the favor of the pope. Stalin laughed as he replied: "The pope! How many divisions has he got?"

Today, Stalin's kingdom is nowhere to be found. Yet Christ's kingdom remains everywhere, thanks to the many "divisions" of lay people deployed not simply by the pope, but by Christ himself — sent as apostles by their baptism, sent out to win a corner of the kingdom in God's name.

CHAPTER 6

The Kingdom and the Secular

In the unfolding of the kingdom, the laity renews the earth in the name of Christ. Their province is the world. Their character, according to Church teaching, is "secular," from *saeculum*, the Latin word denoting the temporal world as it plays out in history.[18] This was the call of the Second Vatican Council (1962-1965): "The laity, by their very vocation, seek the kingdom of God by engaging in temporal affairs and by ordering them according to the plan of God."[19]

This is not a second-class vocation. It is a genuine share in the kingship of Jesus. Blessed John Paul II beautifully expressed the dignity of the lay vocation: "In choosing to live the common life of humanity, the Son of God conferred a new value on this life, raising it to the heights of the divine. Since he is God, he introduced even the humblest activities of human existence to a participation in the divine life. In him we can and must recognize and honor God, who as man was born and lived like us. He ate, drank, worked and did what everyone must do, so that the mystery of the Trinitarian life is reflected in all of life, in all human activities raised to a higher level. For whoever lives in the light of faith, as lay Christians, the mystery of the Incarnation also penetrates temporal activities, imbuing them with the leaven of grace."[20]

What does it mean for us to reflect "the mystery of Trinitarian life"? It means that we are baptized into Christ, and so we spend our days in close communion with our loving Father, and we are faithful to the promptings of the Holy Spirit. We are God's temple now. We are sanctuaries of God's presence. When we live faithfully, our actions represent the actions of the divine king within the kingdom, which has begun in our world.

The mission of the laity is to do all things as Christ would, and so raise their work and their workplaces up to a new level. As St. John Chrysostom put it, we all have the opportunity to make earth into heaven, beginning with our most immediate surroundings.

Some people will be surprised to hear the laity's sacred calling described as having a "secular character." We have been conditioned by our media to see "sacred" and "secular" as opposites. Perhaps this is the inevitable linguistic consequence of our country's constitutional separation of church and state. But it is not true to Christian doctrine, which sees God as sovereign over all things and calls us to be faithful to Christ in every aspect of our lives. "Whatever you do," said St. Paul, "do everything for the glory of God" (1 Cor 10:31). To do otherwise is to be a hypocrite, whose words and actions do not line up.

Some people hold that religious principles should have no place whatsoever in public discourse. They say that any invocation of divine authority will inevitably be an imposition. After all, who can argue with God?

Yet Christians believe that conversion must never be coerced. So we do not impose our beliefs on anyone. We propose the ways of the kingdom in terms that the world can understand and examine, terms they may freely accept or reject.

We have inherited a rich tradition of thoughtful reflection about society, culture, and law. I would like to examine just a few elements of Catholic social doctrine, the elements that are most useful for us as we all seek to answer our divine vocation — so that we all might seek first the kingdom.

Human dignity. God created each and every human being in the divine image and likeness. This means that every person has an infinite value that transcends all circumstances, possessions, and qualities. Our value doesn't vary according to our personal wealth, or our status in society, or our abilities or disabilities. We possess human dignity as long as we have life, from the moment of conception till natural death. We are all equal in the sight of God, who made us and has given us everything that we have.

Sin. We believe that God made us "very good" (Gn 1:31), but from the beginning we have chosen to sin against that goodness. Our first parents committed the "original sin," which weakened them in a grave and deadly way and inclined them and their offspring to commit further sins: what we call "actual sins." These sins are corrosive to human relationships and divisive in human society. When we consider social issues, we must always keep in mind the effects of sin. Nevertheless, in spite of these transgressions, human beings remain essentially good, as God made us.

Universal care. God desires all human beings to be saved, and so our concern is universal. Everyone who is not yet baptized into the kingdom remains a potential fellow citizen of heaven.

Deeds of mercy. When Jesus portrays the final judgment of humanity (Mt 25:31-46), he shows the king rewarding those who fed the hungry, gave drink to the thirsty, welcomed strangers, clothed the naked, and visited those who were sick or imprisoned. Those who refused or neglected to do these works receive a sentence of everlasting punishment. Thus we see that our actions *in this world* have everlasting consequences for our life in the kingdom. So does our inaction! In the pre-Christian pagan world, the poor were considered "losers." In the Christian world they are considered "blessed" (Lk 6:20), and all Christians are called to be a blessing to them.

The common good. It is human nature to live in society. We favor, therefore, a social order that fosters full development (spiritual and temporal) for all human persons. Jesus said: "I came so that they might have life and have it more abundantly" (Jn 10:10).

Solidarity. This principle recognizes that each person, as a member of society, is interconnected with the destiny of all other members of society. For a Christian, this is the simple recognition that all of humanity belongs to the same family. We share the same origin and destiny. We are created, redeemed, and loved by the same God.

Freedom of conscience and freedom of religion. People should be free to express their views, do what they think is morally right, and refuse what they consider to be morally wrong.

Universal destination of goods. The goods of the earth were made for the enjoyment of all humanity. The Church affirms the right of private property, but that right is subordinate to the common good.

All these principles, taken together, do not add up to a political platform. That's not the business of the Church, whose primary concern is for the spiritual good of all people.

These principles provide a useful tool, however, for Catholics who wish to evaluate the policies of candidates and parties. *We should ask: Do they respect the dignity of all human life? Do they*

honor conscience, or do they wish to regulate the freedom of families?
Do they care less for the common good than the privileges of a few?

———

The Church has drawn out these principles systematically in many forms, especially over the last century and a half. It was the Church that offered the first thoughtful reflection on conditions arising from the Industrial Revolution in the nineteenth century. It was the popes who supported the formation of labor unions and affirmed the rights of workers, and it was the Church that warned the world of the dangers of Marxist collectivism.

These principles have been developed at great length, and in their most authoritative form, in the papal letters known as the "social encyclicals." A serious student of Catholic thought will want to study them:

Pope Leo XIII, *Rerum Novarum: On the Condition of Workers* (1891)

Pope Pius XI, *Quadragesimo Anno: On the Reconstruction of the Social Order* (1931)

Pope John XXIII, *Mater et Magistra: Mother and Teacher* (1961)

Pope Paul VI, *Populorum Progressio: On the Development of People* (1967)

Pope John Paul II, *Laborem Exercens: On Human Work* (1981); *Sollicitudo Rei Socialis: On the Twentieth Anniversary of Populorum Progressio* (1987); *Centesimus Annus: The Hundredth Anniversary of Rerum Novarum* (1991)

Pope Benedict XVI, *Caritas in Veritate: Love in Truth* (2009)

We are privileged also to have the teachings digested and arranged in an authoritative, thematic form in the Church's

Compendium of Social Doctrine. This volume is an excellent resource for those who wish to form their conscience, but lack the time for extensive research.

The principles of Catholic social thought are inherently attractive, and at least two recent U.S. presidents (one Republican and one Democrat) have testified to their influence. What's more, they are proven components of a just and peaceful society.

Christians should be free to promote these ideas that we derive from God's revelation. We need not propose them in religious terms. We believe they accord well with nature; for the same God who created the world has revealed the divine order to us. With every commandment, with every act of creation, God wills our happiness and our good, as individuals and as societies.

The kingdom of heaven abides wherever this God is present — present in the people who stand up for the divine law and the natural law established in creation.

What abides when God is absent? Well, God is *never* absent. But human beings, and even entire societies, can choose to ignore his presence. In God's absence, there is no transcendent value. The ultimate value becomes power, usually achieved by money, military might, social status, or physical beauty. Scripture tells us that "the Lord hears the cry of the poor," but apart from the Lord people are too self-absorbed to give their attention to the needs of the vulnerable, the less fortunate, the less attractive.

When Catholic lay people live up to their calling, God's presence is palpable in society. The signs are everywhere: in justice, in peace, in happy families and caring neighborhoods, in citywide safety nets, and in respectful speech.

To live this way is an exercise of priesthood. For the laity are indeed anointed to exercise a "royal priesthood" (1 Pt

2:9). The kingdom we live in is a kingdom of priests (Rv 1:6). When I offer Mass, I lift up the body and blood of Jesus Christ for the sanctification of his Church. But lay people also make an offering: they lift up the world. When they do this, they work to restore all things in Christ (see Eph 1:10), renewing all things, redeeming the time.

This is the good of the kingdom, but it is also the fulfillment of the world.

CHAPTER 7

Standing for the Kingdom

As Americans we have been fortunate in a nation that prides itself on its many freedoms. We sing that we are "the land of the free and the home of the brave," and we have every right to make that claim. Religious freedom is something we tend to take for granted. If we wish to proclaim the kingdom of heaven, we are free to do so. Our fellow citizens are free to accept or reject what we say, but they must honor our right to speak as we wish.

It's a right guaranteed in our Constitution, whose First Amendment begins with the words: "Congress shall make no law respecting an establishment of religion, or prohibiting the free exercise thereof." This part of the Bill of Rights, which was ratified in 1791, has woven the idea of freedom of religion into the fabric of our democracy.

Few Americans may know that statutory religious freedom began on this continent more than one hundred fifty years earlier in the only Catholic English-speaking colony: Maryland. In a historic action, the assembly of this newly formed civil government declared freedom of conscience and free exercise of religion to be the law of the land.

Within thirty years, however, that provision was revoked. In 1704, in an effort to silence Catholics, the new government in Maryland — now controlled by non-Catholics — revoked the statute that provided religious liberty and ordered Catholic churches locked so that, in the words of the governor, they "could never again serve as a place of Catholic worship."

In 2009, I had the pleasure of participating in a ceremony in historic Old St. Mary's City in southern Maryland for the "unlocking" of the first Catholic Church in the English colonies.

You can imagine my delight when I joined the current sheriff of St. Mary's County, arguably the successor to the sheriff who was ordered to lock the chapel, as he inserted a replica of the original key in to the restored chapel's door, and both of us pushed open the door. I could not help but remind the large crowd of participants at this event that it is easy to lock doors, but it is far better to push doors open, to allow a place for vibrant religious faith in the public life of our nation.

Religious faith has provided the impetus for so many of the movements for civic reform and renewal in the United States: the abolitionist movement, which worked for the eradication of slavery; the labor movement; the child-welfare movement; the civil-rights movement; the peace movement(s); the pro-life movement. All of these began, at least in part, as shared crusades or missions advanced by like-minded believers. They grew because they made the case for the kingdom in terms that were appealing even to their co-religionists. As a young Catholic, I was inspired by newspaper photos of priests and nuns, in their distinctive garb, marching against segregation in the cities of the southern states. As a somewhat older Catholic, I am today inspired by the tens of thousands of young people who throng the nation's capital each year, in the dead of winter, for the Mass and Rally for Life and later for the March for Life.

———

These movements were dependent upon religious principle, and they were made possible by religious freedom — a freedom that today is under substantive, though sometimes subtle, challenge.

In some very influential circles, opinion based on religious conviction is no longer welcome. Freedom of religion and freedom of conscience have, in effect, been reduced to freedom to worship within one's own house of prayer — as long as we check our convictions at the door on our way out.

How much has changed in our country! We may be tempted to think that what happened at St. Mary's Chapel in 1704 could not happen now. Yet, quite recently, the Connecticut legislature introduced a law that, in effect, was the same measure. It mandated that the ownership of all Catholic Church property would be removed from the control of the bishop.

More recently still, Professor Kenneth Howell was fired from the University of Illinois at Urbana-Champaign simply for stating the Catholic doctrines on marriage and on homosexuality — in a course about Catholicism! According to news reports, an unidentified student in his class complained that Howell was "limiting the marketplace of ideas and acting out of accord with this institution's mission and principles." Apparently, "academic freedom" ensures that a professor may teach any view of marriage except the view held in common by all cultures until very recently. What was once hallowed as tradition is now vilified as "hate speech." The university's rationale was basically that political correctness should now take precedence over religious freedom and academic freedom.

We are in the midst of a sea change. We are being told that religion has no place in the public forum. Legislatures and courts are being asked to create and apply hate-language legislation directed to faith bodies that dare to challenge politically correct positions. We are told that activists may redefine institutions and conventions as they please — marriage, adoption, health care, and so on — but any principled challenge to those redefinitions is labeled "discrimination."

This aversion to religion plays itself out in absurd ways. In the aftermath of the attacks of September 11, 2001, state and local officials in Pennsylvania hastily organized a memorial service for the families of the heroic passengers on United Airlines Flight 93, which had crashed near the town of Shanksville. Clergy were invited to speak — a priest, a rabbi, and several ministers — but, strangely, they were exhorted by a government official not to mention God in their remarks lest they embroil everyone in a "church-state problem." The young priest, whom I have known since his seminary days, was not deterred. He began his remarks by saying: "Two thousand years ago, Jesus Christ came among us to tell us how we deal with such a tragedy and how we can begin to make sense of it."

One by one after him, the other religious leaders also spoke welcome words of vision and comfort to the mourners and others present who had gathered precisely out of their own religious convictions. Whatever reason the government officials had for organizing the event, the people who actually showed up were there because they knew that religion offered them the only effective way to begin to deal with such horror and evil. (If you read the public addresses of George Washington and Abraham Lincoln, you'll see that such sensibilities are hardly new and hardly un-American.)

Attempts at censorship are often advanced as measures intended to "protect" the people against any encroachment of religion upon secular power. But their effect is quite different; their effect is itself a denial or suppression of many freedoms: freedom of conscience, freedom of religion, freedom of expression, freedom of the (religious) press, and academic freedom. Moreover, they do not serve the interests of "the people," who are typically sympathetic to religion, but rather the interests of an elite who find little use for traditional religion and morality. Such forces will sometimes focus their efforts on the Catholic Church simply because it's the largest religious target, the best organized, and the church most capable of opposing their redefinition of terms and institutions such as marriage, family, and health care.

———

It should be obvious that this is a growing problem.

It is not enough, however, that we recognize the problem and lament its consequences. We must also be prepared to respond to it. How do we begin to fix what is clearly broken?

Today, the new word for defense is "witness."

"The truth is great," goes the old saying, "and it will prevail." But for the truth to prevail it must first be heard. And for it to be heard, it must be spoken.

Faithful members of the Church must find ways of communicating reliable information — the rest of the story — so that the public may know what the facts truly are.

So much of what we receive by way of information is mediated. What we learn comes to us through the filter of a website, with its peculiar prejudices; a newspaper, with its multiple layers of reporter, writer, editor, and publisher; a radio announcer, editor, and producer; or a television reporter, anchor, editor, and producer. What reaches us is what several other people have decided we should know — what they've decided not to filter out.

Media begin, oftentimes, with a predetermined story line. The plot then becomes the norm of selectivity for what goes into the story and all follow-up articles. On a particular issue, is the Church a threatened minority whose voice should be heard with respect — or a reactionary element resisting enlightenment and progress? The headline writer decides.

The story line is not, and cannot be, value-neutral. When editors choose which details will appear in a seven-hundred-word story — or a forty-second radio slot — they are making value judgments about what's important and what's not. Their selection will inevitably reflect their political orientation or that of their employers. I am not the first to observe that the reportage at CNN and at Fox, at the *New York Times* and at the *Wall Street Journal*, is quite obviously slanted toward a particular viewpoint, clearly favoring one party over another, one worldview over another. All of this highlights the need for the faithful to seek unencumbered, unmediated access to "the rest of the story."

I could multiply examples of news media crossing the line from fact to spin in such a way that they create a fog of misinformation. For example: the District of Columbia, where I live, recently passed legislation approving same-sex "marriage." At the public hearings when this legislation was introduced, representatives of the archdiocese and Catholic Charities pointed out that without religious exemption — an exemption granted in every other jurisdiction where similar legislation had been proposed — the legislation would render the Church incapable of continuing some of its programs that serve the needy. There is no way the Church could have complied with every aspect of the new law's sweeping demands.

The next day the local daily ran a front-page story with the headline "Church Gives D.C. Ultimatum." It framed the Church's protest as a threat to the District: "if the city doesn't change the proposed same-sex marriage law," the Church would discontinue social-service programs that could affect tens of thousands of people, including the homeless.

Many people, most of whom derived their information from that newspaper, simply assumed that the Church had taken this position — spitefully, using the poor as a bargaining chip. Soon it was being repeated on radio talk shows: Church uses the poor as a weapon against struggling minorities.

The real story was the clash of rights. The newly created "right" to a newly defined "gay marriage" needed to be balanced with the longstanding right of conscience that has traditionally been protected by religious exemption. The media never covered the real story. They had their own story to tell, and Catholics were cast as the villains.

Another example, and they are legion: The *New York Times* ran a long series of articles attacking Pope Benedict XVI and purporting to survey his years as a Vatican official as well. It announced that while priests were abusing young people, then-Cardinal Joseph Ratzinger ignored his responsibilities in this area, and instead spent his time "publicly disciplining priests in Brazil and Peru for preaching that the Church should work to empower the poor and the oppressed." With nothing to sustain this accusation other than the bald statement by the writer across two full pages of print, the pope was painted as simultaneously a supporter of abusive priests and an oppressor of good priests.

Yet another example: a major newspaper ran a long, long story on the defense of embryonic stem-cell research, carefully avoiding the distinction between embryonic and adult stem-cell research, one of which is moral and the other immoral (and one of which, the moral one, is far more effective than the other). The paper then proceeded to attribute to embryonic stem-cell research the benefits that have been derived solely from adult stem-cell research. For a person unaware of the distinctions and the facts, the newspaper's myth became reality.

So much of what we and our neighbors know about the Catholic Church is mediated through the lens of others, many of whom are simply ignorant of or hostile to the Catholic Church. Recently, PBS ran a documentary titled "God in America," purporting to be a balanced study of the influence of faith in shaping U.S. history and molding the national char-

acter. Early on, the series obsessed about a disastrously unsuccessful Franciscan-led effort to evangelize the pueblos of New
Mexico. The event was uncharacteristic even for its times, and
it is hardly representative of the history of religious people in
America. But the script treated it as iconic, and the writers
naively applied modern values to judge pre-modern events.

Bleached out of the documentary are the stories of the
works of thousands and thousands of men and women religious who educated millions of some of the poorest children in
our nation . . . the thousands of health care and social-service
institutions, hospitals, orphanages, asylums, homes for the aged
that were and are substantial threads throughout the fabric of
our nation . . . the impact of Catholic social teaching on the
efforts of organized labor in the 1920s, 1930s, and 1940s, and
the work of the Church to bring about just legislation governing child labor, decent working conditions, and fair wages
and hours. All these historical contributions are passed over in
silence.

A few years ago, Catholic Charities, USA celebrated its
centenary. In that hundredth year alone, the organization
pointed out that it had assisted nine million people across the
country. That's more than a program. That's an infrastructure.
That's a real safety net to a large percentage of the population.
Yet this somehow was not part of the story of God in America.

What is distressing — and what does as much disservice to
the truth as these just-cited examples — is the silence observed
in the rest of the public media. It is rare that we see even one
news outlet, particularly among the print media, correcting
misinformation in other media.

———

Quite recently I was invited to give the invocation at the
ground-breaking for the new National Law Enforcement

Museum. I was scheduled to speak immediately following the national anthem, and so I was standing backstage waiting for my cue. In the same area sat a young man responsible for controlling the light and sound systems. His was not an easy task. He had an elaborate script in front of him, below a console of rows and rows of audiovisual controls.

A voice announced the presentation of the colors and the singing of our national anthem. The entire audience stood and began to sing.

With the opening bars, I watched that young man do something beautiful. He struggled to put aside his papers and disengage himself from the console, so that he, too, could stand — even though he was seen by no one but me, and he wasn't even aware that I could see him. He stood because the song was our national anthem. He stood because that hymn meant something profound to him.

You and I will also face many moments when we must choose to stand or not to stand. Will we stand up for the Church? Will we, with our words and our actions, tell the story of the kingdom? Will we show the kind of integrity that man displayed — his gestures corresponding to his deepest convictions, whether or not anyone was there to notice him?

You and I will face many moments when we must — quietly, personally, individually, sometimes alone — stand as a defender of the faith, stand as a witness to the truth. We must always speak the truth in love. But we must not remain silent. We must stand up when the kingdom, the Church, the faith, the truth is attacked, belittled, misrepresented, or ignored. Individually and collectively, quietly or insistently, Christians are called to stand for Christ and his kingdom.

CHAPTER 8

Ambassadors for the Kingdom

"Pittsburgh!"

If I close my eyes I can still hear that name resound as if from a distance — from down a corridor or across a room. It was the name by which Blessed John Paul II identified me.

My acquaintance with the Holy Father predated his papacy. I first met him when he was Archbishop of Kraków, Poland, and I was working in the Vatican Congregation for the Clergy. I got to know him because he enjoyed practicing his English with native English-speakers. To the end of his life, he spoke English well, but with an accent, which made my nickname all the more endearing.

Why did he call me "Pittsburgh"? He had several good reasons. He knew it as the city where I'd been born and raised. He had visited the city himself in the 1960s and had great affection for its people. And it was he who named me bishop of my home diocese in 1988.

Thus I was easily identified with "Pittsburgh." To him, my face recalled the Church in my city, the people of that city. To the man entrusted with the keys to the kingdom of heaven, I personified a particular corner of the realm. When he showed affection to me, I knew it was directed beyond me: to my people, to our people, to God's people back home. On my return, I took great pleasure in relaying his greetings and blessing to "Greater Pittsburgh," the city and the surrounding counties.

Wherever I go in the world, my words and my deeds are not simply my own. They represent the Church, especially the Church I serve as bishop, and the same principle applies to every bishop. Once I represented the Church of Pittsburgh. Now I represent the Church of Washington.

I am intensely aware of it, especially as I travel and find myself among people who do not know me. To them, at first, I am the priest in the next seat on the plane — just another stranger about whom they will form their first impressions. When they realize I am a bishop, they may project their impressions onto the Church I represent.

For me, it comes with the job. But it's not just *my* job, or even primarily *my* job. It's your job, too. Remember what I pointed out in an earlier chapter: we share in the apostolate. Thus we are "sent." That's the root meaning of the word *apostle*. We are sent as ambassadors for the kingdom to the world at large.

An ambassador lives in a country not her own. She tries to live as a law-abiding resident of that country. She may live there for many years and raise a family there. She may come to love the country and its people, and forge deeper friendships than she had at home.

Yet an ambassador will always be living a sort of exile — as a stranger in a strange land. She will always be viewed as a representative of the country where she holds citizenship. She represents that country's ideals, virtues, priorities, laws, commerce, and customs.

We should learn from such a life. "Our citizenship is in heaven" (Phil 3:20), though we are ambassadors here on earth. We wait in joyful hope for the day of the kingdom's coming, but meanwhile we love the place where we reside and especially the people who live there. We work to make the world a better place — though our primary allegiance is to Christ the King. We are ambassadors for heaven's kingdom, sent to a particular family, a particular neighborhood, a particular workplace. In those places, we represent Jesus — we *re-present* him — and all the policies and principles of his kingdom.

Ambassadors are also known as diplomats, so their particular way of speaking is called *diplomatic*. They practice *diplomacy*.

We're called to do the same. No matter our topic — no matter our audience — our speech should be marked by the characteristic virtue of the kingdom of heaven: charity. Charity, we know from St. Paul, is "is patient . . . kind . . . not jealous . . . not pompous . . . not inflated . . . it is not rude, it does not seek its own interests, it is not quick-tempered, it does not brood over injury, it does not rejoice over wrongdoing but rejoices with the truth. It bears all things, believes all things, hopes all things, endures all things" (1 Cor 13:4-7).

Just as Blessed John Paul II always spoke English with a winsome Polish accent, we citizens of the kingdom should always speak with a charitable accent. Patience and kindness, humility and understanding should be our distinguishing marks.

———

This may prove challenging. Public discourse has grown coarser over the last half-century. Media trying to scoop their competition routinely invade the privacy of public figures. Photographers hound celebrities and even the children of celebrities. Newspaper reporters have hacked into cell-phone voicemails. The front pages of newspapers and magazines are crowded with stories that are really none of anybody's business.

Where once public figures debated serious issues, they now battle with "sound bites" — slogans designed to provoke strong feelings while communicating little or no information.

Language, moreover, has grown increasingly vulgar, and mainstream media outlets have become channels of obscene and crude speech. A favorite newsman of mine has referred to this phenomenon as "the slobbing of America." In many instances, it's not just the language that's degenerate, but also what is said or implied about others, with nothing more for evidence than an individual's strong emotions.

Since we are immersed in media, it's not surprising that this coarsening has also affected the way we treat one another at work, at school, at home, and even at church. Like muck-raking reporters we can tend to cast our own petty conflicts in terms of power politics, or even the grand struggle of Good versus Evil, when we're really just caught up in an ordinary human misunderstanding or disagreement.

We need to examine the media we consume. We need to be critical consumers. And, when it's necessary, we need to stop consuming the specific media that lead us into bad or even sinful habits of speech or thought.

But, more important, we need to examine how we talk, because we ourselves are media. As ambassadors of God's king-dom, we need — with every word and gesture — to live out our commitment. We need to be a people of profound respect for the truth. Yes, we have a right to express our thoughts, opinions, and positions. Indeed, we who follow Christ are *duty-bound* to speak the truth, but always with charity, always "in love" (Eph 4:15). It is not enough that we know or believe something to be true. We must express that truth with kindness and with true concern for others, so that the bonds between us can be strengthened in building up the Body of Christ.

This is especially true when we find ourselves in disagree-ment with our fellow Catholics. We should always remember that each of us is a temple of the Holy Spirit. Our baptism into Christ creates among us the bonds of a new spiritual family.

Each and every member of the family must ensure that our conversation "at home" proceeds in a manner that not only achieves the ends desired, but also recognizes everyone's rights and dignity. It would be a tragedy to accept as a principle of discourse that the end justifies the means — so that "winning" would validate any destructive behavior or speech.

At the same time, the claims of truth must never be forgotten. Falsehood, too, is a sort of spiritual violence, and it is always unacceptable.

Fearful silence is yet another way we can sin against the truth. We must not be afraid to speak up — though always in charity, with true concern for the person listening. St. Paul emphasizes that we must do this when it's convenient and when it's not, in season and out of season (2 Tm 4:2). Cowardly silence can be disastrous in its consequences. Have you ever wondered how the great atrocities of history came to be? How is it that there were concentration camps dedicated to the extermination of people? How could it be that slavery — the reduction of human beings to the status of property — was protected by law? How is it possible that the wholesale destruction of human life can be accepted by society today? When we look at the magnitude of the evil we are dealing with, one wonders how such activities could be accepted by any people anywhere at any time. Silence is the ally of atrocity, and sometimes the silence of individuals is compounded by the means of social communication. The full horror of what is taking place can be presented in such a way that most people remain ignorant of what is really happening. Silence and ignorance are twin allies of atrocities.

The New Testament places before us the dual demands of truth and charity. They are not contradictory. They must be kept in careful balance. St. Peter puts it beautifully: *"Always be ready to give an explanation* to anyone who asks you for a reason for your hope, *but do it with gentleness* and reverence, keeping your conscience clear, so that, when you are maligned, those who defame your good conduct in Christ may themselves be put to shame" (1 Pt 3:15-16).

We should keep in mind that every adversary is a potential friend — even the most anti-Christian kind. The ninth chapter of the Acts of the Apostles can be instructive for us. There we meet the classic persecutor of the Christian Church: a brilliant and murderous man named Saul of Tarsus. When the Lord told certain Christians that Saul was going to be heaven's "chosen instrument" for spreading the Gospel, the disciples worried that God's omniscience might be slipping, so they subtly reminded him about all the "evil things" Saul had done. God knew, however, that Saul's sins could be overcome by divine grace. Indeed, Saul would become the most dynamic and effective of all the apostles: he would become St. Paul.

This is not something we would have figured out on our own, so God inspired its inclusion in Scripture.

———

"Every good Christian ought to be more ready to give a favorable interpretation to another's statement than to condemn it. But if he cannot do so, let him ask how the other understands it. If the latter understands it badly, let the former correct him with love."[21] That statement comes with the authority of the *Catechism*, invoking the words of St. Ignatius Loyola. It sets out our standard in clear terms, suitable for a daily examination of conscience.

We need to reflect *regularly* on how we engage in discourse and how we live out our commitment as members of the Church and ambassadors for the kingdom.

Even within the Church we may disagree with a decision made by our pastor or our bishop — decisions about policies or procedures — and we speak our mind. But we should speak with a presupposition of the other person's good will, of our shared concern for the Church, and with an awareness that we are all one in faith. Whenever we speak, we are speaking in the presence of the Lord. When we speak within the Church, we are speaking "in Christ" (to use the favorite phrase of St. Paul). Thus, even when we disagree, we strive always to speak the truth in love.

If we do this, we should find it easier, at least within the Church, to arrive at consensus, because it is Christ who calls us together in the first place and it is with his grace that we move forward in conversation.

As Christians we believe that truth itself is strong enough to win the day. We reject the commonplace cynicism of our culture, which tells us: "the one who yells the loudest wins." Truth and charity are the treasury of God's kingdom. Truth and charity should direct all our discussions. Truth and charity will ultimately prevail.

———

We represent the kingdom to a world with which the kingdom is often at odds. We will sometimes, and perhaps often, disagree with the people around us. If we are to be effective as we represent the kingdom, we must learn to disagree in a Christian way.

It bears repeating: we should assume the good will and good intentions of people who disagree with us. They are not necessarily "bigots" and "hate mongers" simply because they hold a position contrary to ours. If we sincerely believe that they do harbor evil intentions, we should remind ourselves of a time when people have misunderstood or misconstrued our own intentions. Then we should call to mind the irrefutable fact that we, too, are occasionally wrong in our judgments.

We should avoid unnecessary hyperbole and, certainly, demagoguery. In a crowd where everyone is screaming, the calm, reasonable, and soft-spoken person will stand out — and possibly win the day. It's not helpful to denounce someone who favors one type of immigration reform as a "traitor" or "unpatriotic." Nor is it proper to say that those who oppose tax credits for inner-city Catholic schools are "bigots," "classists," or "racists." Nor should it be acceptable to dismiss a traditional view of civil marriage as "homophobic" or "discrimination." Labeling other people simply because one disagrees on a specific issue is less than honest and, too often, simply divisive. Good people, and even saints, may disagree in practical matters.

Defamation does more damage to the people who practice it than to the people they scorn. For a Christian, defamation — destroying someone's good name — is a sin that must be confessed and renounced.

Why is charitable, truthful speech so important? Because we do not live alone. While each of us can claim a unique identity, we are, nonetheless, called to live out our lives in relationship with others — in some form of community.

God made us social by nature, and this choice was for a supernatural purpose. All human community brings us, by design, into ever-widening circles of relationship: first with our parents, then with family, then the Church and school and sports teams and musical ensembles and neighborhood associations and, of course, political parties. This is all part of God's plan for bringing us together and keeping us together.

No community, human or divine, political or religious, can exist without trust. At the very core of all human relations is the confidence that members speak the truth to one another. God explicitly protected the bonds of community by prohibiting falsehood as a grave attack on the human spirit: "You shall not bear false witness against your neighbor" (Ex 20:16). To tamper with the truth or, worse yet, to pervert it, is to undermine the foundations of human society and to begin to cut the threads that weave us into a cohesive family.

To speak the truth requires self-discipline and conscious effort. We must search out the facts and avail ourselves of the information necessary to make a judgment based on reality. It is a disservice to the truth when one's opinions, positions, or proposals are based on unverified gossip, unsupported rumor, or partial information. If all the facts are readily available to us, we are obliged to undertake serious study before we pronounce our opinions. This is particularly true if our opinions involve the good name, honor, and integrity of another.

I'm not denying "freedom of speech." Instead, I want to recognize that we have a God-given obligation *to respect the very function of human speech.* We are not free to say whatever we want about another, but only what is true. To the extent that freedom is improperly used — to sever bonds of trust, for example — to that extent, it is irresponsible and not truly free. The commandment that obliges us to avoid false witness also calls us to tell the truth. We ought not to invoke the First Amendment as a license to break the eighth commandment.

Someone once described a "gossip" as a person who will never tell a lie if a half-truth will do as much harm. We should do our best to avoid gossip. When someone begins to "dish" to us "confidentially," we can decline in a polite and friendly way. We can change the subject. When we do this, we are practicing kindness not only toward the person who is the subject of the gossip, but also toward the perpetrator, who has been offered a gentle and oblique reminder that gossip is unseemly and, yes, even at times immoral.

What goes for personal conversation goes double for media consumption. We should take caution and even avoid television shows, publications, or websites that traffic in "scoops," or that "spin" real news into caricatures and conspiracy theories.

There is nothing harmless about gossip or spin. These are like infections that spread sickness throughout the body of society. When they spread through the Church, their perpetrators "will have to answer," as St. Paul said, "for the body . . . of the Lord" (1 Cor 11:27), because the Church, as we've seen, is the Body of Christ.

In our age of blogs and social media, even the wildest accusations can quickly become perceived as "fact." These untruths go unchallenged because the people who are the object of the discussion are usually not present to defend themselves, their views, or their actions.

In all dimensions of our world — whether virtual or real — we need to be ambassadors for Christ and defenders of truth. When we post our comments in the media at our disposal — and we really should do so — we should make our words an occasion of grace, a manifestation of God's kingdom.

———

There is a place for correction and reproof in Christian conversation, and sometimes we must use strong words. In our tradition there is even a place for techniques such as satire and parody, which the saints — from Irenaeus in the second century to Thomas More in the sixteenth — knew how to employ for the appropriate occasions. Yet even with our strongest words we should show that we genuinely care about the other person.

A wise and ancient Catholic maxim has always instructed us to "hate the sin and love the sinner." Yes, some actions are clearly wrong. Yet we must distinguish between *what* is done and *who* does it. The *action* is evil. The *person* is good, created in goodness by almighty God. Those who commit evil deeds sin against their deepest selves when they sin against God. That's the fact we must demonstrate to sinners.

We have an obligation to witness, but there's only one way to witness effectively, and it's not the way of spin, or gossip, or insult. It's not always an easy way, but it's the only way forward. It's the only way that works, and there's ample proof of that.

Our Catholic *faith* is tough. It has had to be tough to survive twenty difficult centuries — when no other institution has survived that long.

Our *hope* is strong, and it's reasonable. After all, the faith that has prevailed through twenty centuries is likely to triumph in our little lifetime. We have good reasons to hope.

This faith and hope are facts of history, not spin. They're durable and they're true. But there's something even stronger than our faith and hope, and more durable still. It's charity: "faith, hope, love remain, these three; but the greatest of these is love" (1 Cor 13:13).

Only if our lives and speech proclaim this love are they truly Christian and truly representative of the Church and the kingdom.

CHAPTER 9

Re-Proposing the Kingdom

What, then, stands in the way of the kingdom? If Christ has already won the victory, why must we wait for his promises to be fulfilled?

If we consult the *Catechism* we learn that God's kingdom is up against some formidable foes. "The triumph of Christ's kingdom will not come about without one last assault by the powers of evil."[22] "The kingdom will be fulfilled . . . only by God's victory over the final unleashing of evil . . . God's triumph over the revolt of evil will take the form of the Last Judgment after the final cosmic upheaval of this passing world."[23]

It sounds very dramatic and even sensational. Terms like "cosmic upheaval" suggest, perhaps, one of the battle scenes from the *Star Wars* epic.

Well, the upheaval is cosmic, and the drama is real; but the battlefield is not in a galaxy far, far away. It's actually quite close to home. The battle is cosmic, but it is waged in the human heart.

The kingdom's obstacles are not force fields or light sabers, but something much more powerful: humanity's power of free will, and our inclination to sin, selfishness, and vice.

Those are the true enemies of the kingdom: anything that turns us in on ourselves; anything that turns us away from acknowledging others, understanding others, and serving others; anything that encourages us to make our own desires supreme over everything. For that is the very essence of idolatry: to offer sacrifice, to give our lives, to something less than God.

Humanity's temptations vary from one historical period to the next, and from one place on the globe to another, but they do tend to coalesce around that famous short list of transgressions, the seven deadly sins. They are: wrath, greed, sloth, lust, envy, gluttony, and (deadliest of all) pride.

As long as we are living on this earth, we must struggle against these. Some of these may occupy us differently at different times of our lives. Some of them may trouble us not at all. But if we say they have no hold on us whatsoever, we're probably being less than honest with ourselves, and in fact convicting ourselves of the sin of pride!

"If we say, 'We are without sin,' we deceive ourselves, and the truth is not in us" (1 Jn 1:8). I don't think St. John was talking about unusual people here. I suspect that self-deception is common, if not epidemic. I suspect that our tendency is to live in denial of the conditions on the battlefield, since we are facing an enemy invincible against our weakened nature.

But St. John anticipated our discouragement and quickly pointed out the way to victory: "If we *acknowledge* our sins, he is faithful and just and will forgive our sins and cleanse us from every wrongdoing" (1 Jn 1:9). This is a ringing endorsement for the value of the spirit of penance that Catholics have always prized. This is why we go to the sacrament of confession — because there we can acknowledge our sins, freely gain forgiveness from God, and walk away clean. This is why we undertake a spiritual workout, a supernatural training program, every year during Lent. God gives us the grace we need to win each battle for the kingdom. Without his grace, we cannot win. In fact, apart from his grace, we are sure to lose.

What are the sins that most beset us? Only you, working with your confessor, can answer that question for you. Only I, working with my confessor, can answer that question for me.

There are, however, sins and temptations that seem to settle on a culture, on a society, at a particular time. They are like storms that arise from the convergence of several fronts on a weather map.

I believe we, especially in America and its cultural satellites, face several serious obstacles as we struggle to bring about the kingdom of God. They are our particular issues, peculiar to our time and place. They are the result of many historical forces — social and industrial revolutions, the spread of democracy, technological advances, the rise of mass media and instant communications, and widespread affluence.

These things in themselves are not bad, and in fact can be quite good and godly. But they can also be fashioned into idols: when people make them absolute rather than relative, when people set them up as supreme goods, in place of God, when people insist that these things must be had and honored at any cost.

When that happens on a large scale, a culture can become so opposed to the good that it can rightly be called a "culture of death." It becomes an anti-kingdom.

Over the course of a long lifetime, Pope Benedict XVI has pondered the moral maladies of western culture. He grew up amid the horrors of the Nazi regime in Germany. He spent his young adulthood in the increasingly secularist Europe of the postwar years. He watched the destructive ideologies of communism and fascism compete for people's minds and hearts. Then he observed the moment that some people called the "end of history," as many people tired of ideologies and collapsed entirely into themselves.

In looking at the current state of western culture, Pope Benedict has diagnosed a complex condition that leaves us weak, dissipated, and helpless against our moral enemies. In a speech delivered in Washington, D.C., in April 2008, he noted that Americans in particular should focus on three insidious "isms." They are, he said, "barriers" to our encounter with Christ. As such, they are obstacles to the kingdom.

1. Secularism. After praising our country as "a land of great faith," the Holy Father noted that "the subtle influence of secularism can nevertheless color the way people allow their faith to influence their behavior. Is it consistent to profess our beliefs in church on Sunday, and then during the week to promote business practices or medical procedures contrary to those beliefs? Is it consistent for practicing Catholics to ignore or exploit the poor and the marginalized, to promote sexual behavior contrary to Catholic moral teaching, or to adopt positions that contradict the right to life of every human being from conception to natural death? Any tendency to treat religion as a private matter must be resisted. Only when their faith permeates every aspect of their lives do Christians become truly open to the transforming power of the Gospel."

2. Materialism. "For an affluent society, a further obstacle to an encounter with the living God lies in the subtle influence of materialism, which can all too easily focus the attention on the hundredfold, which God promises now in this time, at the expense of the eternal life which he promises in the age to come (cf. Mk 10:30). People today need to be reminded of the ultimate purpose of their lives. They need to recognize that implanted within them is a deep thirst for God. They need to be given opportunities to drink from the wells of his infinite love. It is easy to be entranced by the almost unlimited possibilities that science and technology place before us; it is easy to make the mistake of thinking we can obtain by our own efforts the fulfillment of our deepest needs. This is an illusion. Without God, who alone bestows upon us what we by ourselves cannot attain (cf. *Spe Salvi*, 31), our lives are ultimately empty. People need to be constantly reminded to cultivate a relationship with him who came that we might have life in abundance (cf. Jn 10:10)."

3. Individualism. "In a society which values personal freedom and autonomy, it is easy to lose sight of our dependence on others as well as the responsibilities that we bear toward them. This emphasis on individualism has even affected the Church (cf. *Spe Salvi*, 13-15), giving rise to a form of piety which sometimes emphasizes our private relationship with God at the expense of our calling to be members of a redeemed community. Yet from the beginning, God saw that 'it is not good for the man to be alone' (Gn 2:18). We were created as social beings who find fulfillment only in love — for God and for our neighbor. If we are truly to gaze upon him who is the source of our joy, we need to do so as members of the people of God (cf. *Spe Salvi*, 14). If this seems counter-cultural, that is simply further evidence of the urgent need for a renewed evangelization of culture."

Forgive me for quoting the Holy Father at length, but I have seen no better summary of our current difficulties. Through the Church, Christ scatters seed upon American soil that is dry, rocky, and sown with weeds — soil that has built up a certain resistance to authentic religious experience.

Secularism now pressures us to trust only what we can observe and measure. It claims to destroy the classical and time-tested relationship between faith and reason. In fact, it looks upon religion as the superstitious residue of a past, unenlightened age. There's a problem with that view, however. Reason must rest upon first principles that are ultimately resistant to proof. How do we know, for example, that what we perceive is real? Why should we trust our senses? With no faith to stand on, reason itself soon falls down a rabbit hole as conflicting theories of "rationality" emerge. Welcome to the postmodern world.

Consumerism suggests that our worth is not intrinsic or transcendent, but rather can be tallied up in the possessions we've accumulated. "What's your income?" and "What are you worth?" have become interchangeable questions for many Americans.

Individualism demands that we rely only on ourselves — that we owe nothing to anyone else, and that our personal needs should always take first place. This attitude is the antithesis of the virtue of solidarity, and it is incompatible with any kind of charity. Nowhere has individualism had more devastating effects than in the area of human sexuality. The attempt to recast sex as something casual and recreational has crippled marriage and family life and thus weakened the most basic bonds of society. When people fall into individualist ways of thinking, they come to view fidelity as a burden and an impairment. For individualism will accept no restrictions on a person's autonomy — not even the limits imposed by nature. Individualism denies, in fact, that there is any such thing as a common human *nature*, since the *individual* is all that really matters. Thus, according to this view, we may make up our own rules as we go along. Individualism leaves us with what social commentators have called the "cult of self" and the "culture of narcissism." Individualism leads people to put an obsessive focus on their resume, their career, and the next promotion, so that work requires them to be always busy, with no time for family or friends. In this setting it becomes commonplace to treat people as objects to be used for material gain.

These three trends can, and do, dominate and consume the lives of many people. Together, they take on the appearance of a religion: offering an earthly paradise and earthly glory in exchange for a sacrifice of the relationships and commitments that could make someone truly happy on earth: self-giving love, family life, prayer, friendship, detachment from material goods.

Pope Benedict has called the resulting cultural situation a "dictatorship of relativism." If every individual reigns supreme — if every "I" is the sole arbiter of truth — then society's *enemy* becomes the person or institution (or kingdom) that dares to disagree — that dares to say that truth is objective and unchanging, that nature is a teacher, and that morals matter.

In such a world, tradition, true religion, and indeed *all transcendent values* are seen as killjoys and spoilsports — impediments to human progress — that must be suppressed.

———

Just as he diagnosed the problem, so too did Pope Benedict present a practical solution. He has repeatedly summoned the entire Church to a "New Evangelization." He even created a Vatican office whose principal task will be to promote the New Evangelization.

It's fair for us to ask: What's so new about evangelization? After two millennia, hasn't the western world already been evangelized enough? Haven't words like *salvation*, *glory*, *gospel* become like so much white noise to our neighbors?

But the word the Holy Father chose to describe the newness of our effort is itself startlingly new. He's not asking us just to repeat the same old pieties. He calls us to a different task: "to re-propose the perennial truth of Christ's Gospel."

Re-propose — the Italian word is *riproporre*, and is itself an unusual verb in the papal lexicon. Yet there it is, the verbal centerpiece of our new job description.

Pope Benedict wants us to re-propose the kingdom "in the countries where the first proclamation of the faith has already resonated and where churches with an ancient foundation exist but are experiencing the progressive secularization of society and a sort of 'eclipse of the sense of God.'" Does that landscape sound familiar to you? I think I can recognize it, if I look out my window.

We must somehow re-propose the kingdom to those who are convinced that they already know it — and who have already concluded our message is irrelevant. We have to invite them to hear the Gospel all over again, as if for the first time.

Before we can share anything, however, we have to be confident in our message. We can't give away anything if we don't first own it ourselves. We must make an effort to learn the faith, to know Christ deeply through faith, and then to manifest a resulting serenity and happiness in our lives.

Our good lives will serve as a pre-evangelization. Our "secular character," our public integrity, will confirm for our listeners the truth of what they hear us say with our words.

We do need to use words — because that's how humans communicate the things that are truly important. But, again, we must make an effort to find words that truly convey our meaning. No white noise. We're all about re-proposing.

———

I met, not long ago, with a young man and his wife getting ready for the baptism of their baby. Both had been raised Catholic, and the husband indicated that he'd even attended some parish religious-education classes when he was a child. But he also admitted that what he'd been taught didn't mean much to him. Nevertheless, as we talked about the upcoming baptism of his child, he grew attentive. I told him, in plain terms, what the sacrament would do for his son. It's not just a social event, not just a rite of passage. It's a share in Christ's life, a communion with the divine nature. After just a little bit of this, he said with some surprise: "This is like hearing it all over again for the first time."

I had a similar encounter with a young adult seated next to me on a plane. He told me he was going to his niece's first Holy Communion — and he made it clear that this was *not* something he found particularly exciting. "I'm going," he said, "because it's my younger brother's kid and because my mother told me she was really counting on me being there." Like the young father at the baptism, he, too, said he had received some religious instruction during elementary school, but that none of it stayed with him.

So we spent the flight talking about why the event was so important to his mother, and to his niece, and to his brother. What did they see in it? And what, in fact, does the Church teach about it? What really happens at Sunday Mass?

By the end of the flight, the man was visibly excited about the event. What a change! He said to me: "Father, thanks for talking to me. This Holy Communion thing is cool." Then, after a pause, he added, somewhat apologetically, "I mean, *great*."

We all know people like the young couple and the man on the plane. In spite of the genuine and heroic efforts of parents and volunteers in our religious-education programs, sometimes the message simply is not heard the first time around.

The ignorance tends to increase from one generation to the next, as the family dimension of instruction vanishes to nothing. Often today, we in the Church find ourselves teaching the children of under-catechized parents and those children's children. The question arises: Will the next generation see any reason to go to church?

Our educational effort takes place, moreover, in a wider cultural context that is apathetic toward the faith.

All of this, I believe, has created a vast opportunity for lay Catholics to step forward and give witness. A clergyman will see that baby's father once every few years, when his children come forward for the sacraments. But there are Catholics, perhaps many of them, who see him every day — on the subway or the bus to work . . . in the office . . . in the neighborhood as he walks his last blocks home . . . in the gym as he tries to stay in shape . . . on the playground as his kids play with theirs. That's their chance to re-propose the faith to him. Are they taking the chance? Are they re-telling the story? Do they re-propose an encounter with Jesus?

People are ready for such a re-proposal. I saw that in both of these cases, and I can cite many others.

Why am I surprised each time by the openness I find in such people? Could it be that the culture's basic package — secularism, materialism, and individualism — is actually shallow and unsatisfying for most people?

Many centuries ago, there was a young adult named Augustine, who was bright and gifted, successful in a worldly way, and uninterested in the Church's message. Yet when he heard it proposed in a new way, he discovered that it was the answer to his every question, and to every aching need of his heart. He thanked God, saying, "You have made us for yourself, O Lord, and our hearts are restless till they rest in you!" The prayer was echoed many centuries later by a brilliant mathematician named Blaise Pascal, a playboy and a gambler, who heard the Gospel presented with a new voice, by people convinced of its truth, and was converted.

Augustine and Pascal were among the most brilliant men of their times. Yet they were unsatisfied with all that the world offered to their souls. You have the truth that those men lacked and yet could not name. They could not even name their hunger.

How many people are similarly hungry today, and waiting for you to feed them — waiting for you to re-propose their fulfillment?

CHAPTER 10

Kingdom as Conscience

In my work as Archbishop of Washington, D.C., I sometimes pass through the rotunda of the Capitol building. If I have a moment to spare, I like to take a detour through the National Statuary Hall. It's like a forest of sculptures — in bronze, marble, granite, and plaster — all depicting people who contributed to our country's greatness. Each state is invited to contribute two statues of prominent citizens for permanent display. Though its setting is secular, it is still more than a museum. It has something of the qualities of a shrine.

I am proud that so many of the statues in this "Hall of Heroes" depict Catholics. It is obvious in the case of the four priests and one religious sister portrayed there. They appear wearing the distinctive marks of their vocation: St. Damien de Veuster for Hawaii, Blessed Junipero Serra for California, Father Eusebio Kino for Arizona, Father Jacques Marquette for Wisconsin, and Mother Joseph Pariseau for the state of Washington. What did they do? They manifested the kingdom. They manifested the signs Jesus spoke about: healing the sick, preaching the good news to the poor, instructing those who faced limited opportunities for betterment. They founded hospitals, schools, hospices, orphanages, guilds for trades; and they helped to order their communities in a just and peaceful way.

Statues of lay Catholics are not as obvious to a casual browser, since they bear no religious badges or uniforms, but their contributions are no less great. I need mention only Charles Carroll, who signed the Declaration of Independence, and Sacagawea, the native guide of the explorers Lewis and Clark.

These heroes helped to make our nation what it is, and it was their faith that motivated them to labor for excellence. Our country's greatness rests upon the contributions of these men and women of faith. If ever you need a confirmation of this, take a day and drive along the highways of California. You'll trace the missionary itinerary of the long-ago Franciscans. You'll know it by the names of the cities: San Diego, Santa Catalina, San Clemente, San Juan Capistrano, Los Angeles, Santa Monica, Santa Susanna, Santa Barbara, Santa Maria, San Luis Obispo, Guadalupe, San Simeon, Santa Cruz, San Jose, San Francisco . . . To read the road signs is to recite a veritable Litany of the Saints. Catholic faith is woven into the geography as well as the history of that great state.

What's true of California is true of many other places as well — cities where church spires and domes mark the skyline; towns where generations of citizens have been educated in Catholic schools; rural areas where a cemetery suddenly appears among the fields, with its simple monuments proclaiming Catholic doctrine and devotion: the crucifix, the Blessed Virgin, the holy angels.

These images are memorials of the contributions of Catholics to the building of a nation — and they are reminders of the work that Catholics *still* carry on, today, right now, quietly, to bring about the kingdom. What the Church brings to the culture is far more than anyone sees in brick-and-mortar institutions. What the Church offers is the voice of an informed conscience, the prize possession of every believer who strives to live the faith.

What the Catholic Church brings to the world, to our society, is Jesus Christ, his Gospel, his vision, his way of life, and his promise of a kingdom abounding in truth, justice, compassion, kindness, understanding, peace, and love. In the language of our culture we speak of a good and just society, but with the eyes of faith we see God's kingdom coming to be among us.

———

It's not just California. Among the earliest European colonists to arrive in the northeastern states were the pilgrims who landed on the coast of Massachusetts. Before they left their small ship, the Mayflower, they reached an agreement known as the Mayflower Compact. In 1620 these intrepid pioneers sought a life of freedom guided by two principles: the law of God and the common good.

"In the name of God, amen" they began their Compact, the first written articulation of a political philosophy in the English colonies. That document has served as an underpinning for the American political experience for almost four hundred years. At the heart of this formula is the principle that divine law — however it is known — is normative for human action and that civil law should recognize and uphold the common good.

These fundamental principles would underlie an entire tradition of legal development, from The Fundamental Orders in 1639 (which was the first written constitution that set permanent limitations on government power) and the Virginia Bill of Rights (authored by Thomas Jefferson), through the Northwest Ordinance in 1787 (which guaranteed the inhabitants of that territory the same rights and privileges that the citizens of the thirteen states enjoyed). In other chapters we have already mentioned the Declaration of Independence in 1776 and our own United States Constitution in 1787. These documents echo the same theme: we are a free people who recognize the sovereignty of God in our personal and societal life.

Thomas Jefferson stated that the ideals and ideas which he set forth in the Declaration of Independence were not original with him, but were the common opinion of his day. In a letter to Henry Lee, dated May 8, 1825, Jefferson wrote that the Declaration is "intended to be an expression of the American mind and to give that expression proper tone and spirit." Jefferson recognized no distinction between public and private morality. He wrote to James Madison in 1789, "I know but one code of morality for all, whether acting singly or collectively." There is little room in his thought for the idea that one can be personally opposed to gravely wrong actions, but publicly in favor of them.

In all these texts we find certain common threads: the belief that there is an objective moral law, that government must be guided by foundational moral principles, that all human government is fallible and so must be limited, and that God's law is discernible through human reason.

———

The voice of the churches was strong at the time of America's founding, and it remained so for centuries afterward. Religious morality was the engine of reform, whenever reform was needed. The political parties depended upon it. Secular government simply did not have the means to resolve disputes about the personhood of slaves, about equality before the law, and about civil rights. Such matters are utterly dependent on rights that are God-given — or there's no such thing as rights at all.

Once upon a time, our nation took this role for granted. Candidates for office, civil servants, legislators, and bureaucrats all assumed that religion should occupy this place — that it should be the conscience of society.

Today, however, that's not the case, or at least it's not common in certain sectors of media, academia, and government. Where religious values once held sway, many people today look for a secular frame of reference. I welcome these efforts insofar as they might help us better to articulate the natural moral law. Yet many of these efforts are striving for something more — or maybe less — than that worthy goal. Rather than seeking truth and justice in a way that's respectful of religion, today's secularist seeks to bleach religion out of public life. Their goal is to start over — this time without God.

The Church continues to be the one place where such issues can be discussed in a moral framework. We've moved on, however, from the personhood of slaves, and now we must defend the personhood of all humans from conception through gestation and all the way to natural death. The Church remains the conscience of the country as we confront a new range of technological possibilities: abortion, *in vitro* fertilization, embryonic stem-cell research, and physician-assisted suicide. The Church continues to be the place where we consider not just special interests, but the common good; not just opinion polls, but divine law; not just possibility, but morality.

Secular governments simply cannot resolve these profound disputes about right and wrong. The natural law is discernible by all, but only with difficulty, as all human beings are impaired by original sin. Divine law, as we find it in revelation, does not contradict natural law, but clarifies its demands so that they are easier to fulfill, given the weakness of human nature. When people hear the divine law, they often recognize that it accords with the law they find in their conscience. It has the ring of authenticity, the ring of truth.

As Catholics, we look to the Church for guidance that can come only from God. We believe that the teaching of the Church represents for us an opening to the wisdom of God. Our choices in the political arena must be conscientious. Christ promised us he would not leave us orphans. He established his Church as his new body so that his presence would continue with us. He also sent the gift of the Spirit, who would guide us and remind us of all he taught. As members of Christ's Church we look to Catholic doctrine — guided by the Holy Spirit — to help us form our conscience. The bishops are not just one more voice. They speak with Christ's authority. "Whoever listens to you listens to me," Jesus told his apostles (Lk 10:16), and the apostles' successors are the bishops today.

———

When we speak of rights and laws, it's easy for us to get caught up in abstractions, and conscience can seem something theoretical. But our obligations are quite concrete. Lives depend on us. The most vulnerable Americans, whether they know it or not, depend upon faithful Catholics to work and vote according to a well-formed conscience, and to help form a world where they themselves can safely live out their lives in liberty and the pursuit of happiness.

A number of years ago, I had the opportunity to visit a maternity hospital in Peru that was supported and sustained by the Diocese of Pittsburgh. It operated in Chimbote, one of the poorest parts of a country with a large, struggling population of poor and needy people.

I had forgotten how strong a newborn can be. At the invitation of the sisters running the maternity ward, I gingerly picked up a one-day-old infant. The baby was trusting and not shy at all. He latched onto my finger with all his force and held tight. It was as if the baby already knew that his mother, because of her poverty, disability, and many other needs, was going to give him up for adoption. Given to me — given to the Church — he held on with all his strength.

That infant was a parable to me, a parable of the kingdom — a representative of countless unborn infants reaching out to hold onto you and me, reaching out with all their strength. We are the only refuge they have in their struggle to find a place, a home, a life in this world. We are their voice in this nation.

I believe that the current effort to bleach God out of public life will ultimately fail. God is a part of the lives of the majority of people in our nation. This is demonstrated in poll after poll. To pretend otherwise fails to prepare society to deal realistically with the actual human condition. God was with the people who forged this great nation from sea to shining sea. God is still with us today.

The secularist model for public political discourse fails us. Every culture in human history has recognized the deeply human need for a *transcendent authority* to sanction right from wrong. The secular model can't do this. "Secular" means worldly, and secularism simply cannot transcend the world. It cannot transcend itself. And so, with no superior resources, its vitality is limited. Its point of reference has no lasting value.

I remain optimistic. Things are seriously out of kilter, but that is itself a wake-up call to conscience, and I know people are hearing it and heeding it. One particularly encouraging sign is the large number of young people who come to our nation's capital for the Rally and Mass for Life that precedes the March for Life. This past year, the Archdiocese of Washington hosted close to 40,000 youths and young adults whose pro-life energy was evident and whose voices were audible.

Our Holy Father, in his message to them, noted his deep gratitude. His letter from the Cardinal Secretary of State pointed out that he "is deeply grateful to all who take part in this outstanding annual witness to the Gospel of Life . . . He is particularly grateful for the significant representation of young Americans whose generosity, idealism and concern have inspired them to raise their voice on behalf of the most defenseless of our brothers and sisters. Respect for life is essential to the building of a truly just, good and free society, in which each person is accepted as a brother or sister within the great human family (cf. *Caritas in Veritate*, 29)."

To this huge throng now silent, the Holy Father's representative continued: "The Holy Father encourages the young people to rise to this urgent moral challenge. He is confident that they will contribute to the renewal of American society by their witness to the sacredness of God's gift of life and their efforts to ensure that this basic human right is always given adequate legal protection."

We must always be encouraged. God is strong, and the kingdom is his doing. He asks us not to succeed, but to be faithful to him.

We begin with our serene but firm affirmation that God is a part of our life, public and private. When enough people say what they believe, we will be heard.

We should be proud of our history, our heritage, and our faith — all those heroes whose statues stand in the Capitol. More than that, we should be proud to take up their legacy, to do now what they did then — to bring Jesus Christ to the world.

CHAPTER 11

The Voice of the Kingdom

Who speaks for the Catholic Church?

The news media — even the Catholic media — make people ponder the question. In the mail a few weeks ago I received an article that condemned many of the Church's common liturgical practices. The authority for the condemnation was not the pope, not a council of bishops, not even the national conference of bishops, but rather an alleged visionary who claimed to receive messages from heaven. Heaven surely trumps all earthly authority, so the visionary lays claim to speak for the *true* Catholic Church.

In the same mail was a letter challenging the Church's teaching on the indissolubility of the marriage bond and a number of other Catholic doctrines. These, said the correspondent, were products not of the true Church, but of the "institutional Church." The basic thrust of his argument was that he was free to flout the doctrine of the Church because his authority was as good as any institution's.

Who *really* speaks for the Catholic Church? Who speaks for the *true* Church?

The question arose again recently when a Catholic priest, a member of a learned society and professor of theology, arrived in Washington to address any members of Congress who would accept his invitation. He offered an alternative vision of marriage — far different from the doctrine taught by the bishops and the *Catechism* — and he advertised it as authentically Catholic. He did not offer his message as theological speculation or as a classroom exercise of academic freedom, but rather as an alternative and equally Catholic *pastoral* instruction to the faithful.

Who speaks for the Church? In all of these instances, we see people appealing to a supposedly higher authority. In the first case, it is reportedly direct communication with God — over and against the rulings of present and recent popes and councils. In the second case the claim is to private judgment and individual expertise that, in the correspondent's opinion, was sufficient on its own to form conscience and override the direct and explicit teaching of the Church. In the third case, an academic deemed himself the judge of the Church's decisions. In every case, the bottom line is the same: one individual's interpretation of God's word supersedes the role and voice of the bishops.

"Hierarchy" gets a bad rap from popular culture today. Like "kingdom," it is often misunderstood — equated with vestigial aristocracy in traditional societies or superfluous bureaucracy in corporations.

That's not what the Church means by hierarchy. At root, the word means "sacred order." The Church is a society, established by Jesus Christ, and its founder created it with a certain order. In any society, order is a prerequisite for peace and prosperity. This is as true of democracies as it is of kingdoms, and as true in the twenty-first century as it was in the first.

In the very generation of the apostles, St. Clement of Rome witnessed to the need for hierarchy: "Our apostles, too, were given to understand by our Lord Jesus Christ that there would be contention over the office of bishop. For this reason, equipped as they were with perfect foreknowledge, they appointed successors and afterward provided for a continuance, so that if these should fall asleep, other approved men should succeed to their ministry."[24]

The contention goes on. But, in response, the *Catechism of the Catholic Church* devotes an entire section to its discussion of "The Hierarchical Constitution of the Church." Here we read that "Christ is himself the source of ministry in the Church. He instituted the Church. He gave her authority and mission, orientation and goal."[25] The Church received its structure by the will of Christ, and its form is an essential part of the Church he instituted. The New Testament shows us a hierarchical Church, with bishops, presbyters (priests), and deacons. The earliest Christian writers, those we call the "Apostolic Fathers," assume that the Church has this hierarchical form, which we still preserve today.

The *Catechism* goes on to outline how Jesus established the Church on the apostles and gave to Peter a unique and enduring authority. The *Catechism* speaks of the pope as the "perpetual and visible source and foundation of the unity both of the bishops and the whole company of the faithful,"[26] and of the college of bishops composed of all of the bishops throughout the world and of the individual bishops as "the visible source and foundation of unity in their own particular Churches."[27] Following the teaching of the Church, the traditional duties of the bishops are listed as teaching, sanctifying, and governing. In each of these three areas, the bishops, in the local churches or dioceses, together with the pope for the whole Universal Church, speak for the Church.

The *United States Catholic Catechism for Adults* also highlights the role of the bishops as teachers of the faith. We are reminded that, unlike fundamentalists and some evangelicals who hold solely a personal, individual, and literal interpretation of the Bible, Catholics hold that revelation is transmitted by apostolic tradition and Scripture together. "The Church and Apostolic Tradition existed before the written New Testament. Her Apostles preached the Gospel orally before writing it down. The Apostles appointed bishops to succeed them with the authority to continue their teaching."[28]

Why? The answer is found in Jesus' guarantee that the faithful would not be led astray. As the *Catechism* teaches: "In order to preserve the Church in the purity of faith handed on by the apostles, Christ who is the Truth willed to confer on her a share in his own infallibility."[29] Christ chose men as apostles whom he would anoint in the Holy Spirit and guide as they taught and led his Church. They in turn chose successors through the laying on of hands and the imparting of the Spirit to continue this work.

The responsibility of the bishops is to teach in the name of Christ. This authority extends to applying the Gospel to the issues and circumstances of our own day. The faithful, including theologians, may speculate and attempt to understand more deeply the revelation of Our Lord, but such opinion can never replace or equal the authoritative teaching of those to whom Christ himself has entrusted the care of his Gospel.

———

The pastors of the Church, the pope and bishops, have been explicitly charged to guide the faithful in the way of salvation. They are the fixed point in a changing world. Since they are accountable to sacred tradition, they represent objectivity against the subjective claims of many individuals.

There is, of course, a place in the Church for theological speculation and even private revelation. But only the Church's "Magisterium" — its official and divinely conferred teaching authority — can serve as a sure norm to guide us along Christ's way to eternal life.

Once when Jesus was teaching, he spoke of how he intended to give his own Body and Blood for "the life of the world." Some, who found this teaching difficult, disputed it and walked away. As St. John tells us: *"Many* of his disciples, when they heard it, said, 'This saying is hard; who can accept it?'"* (Jn 6:60, emphasis added). But Jesus did not change his teaching because some of the disciples disagreed. He did not amend it. In fact, the Gospel says Jesus repeated it. He affirmed that he intended to give us his own Body and Blood for our salvation. Tragically, the same narrative recounts: "As a result of this, many [of] his disciples returned to their former way of life and no longer accompanied him" (Jn 6:66).

Our Lord did not back down. He is the way, the truth, and the life (see Jn 14:6). He reveals God's plan. We come to him for grace, enlightenment, and redemption. We do not set the rules. We are not the ones who fashion the way in which we are saved, redeemed, and granted a share in the glory of God's kingdom. God takes care of that.

When confronted with dissent, Jesus said to the Twelve, "Do you also want to leave?" Simon Peter, who understood, answered him, "Master, to whom shall we go? You have the words of eternal life. We have come to believe and are convinced that you are the Holy One of God" (Jn 6:67-69).

Christ committed to those apostles the task of preaching his word in his name, that is, *with authority*. He assured them of the help of the Holy Spirit, who would guard them in all truths (see Jn 14:16-26). He commanded them to teach his word to all nations, binding the hearers to the duty of believing their words as the word of God, and he promised to be with them in their preaching until the end of time (see Mt 28:20).

The bishops are the successors of the apostles. They are not just one more voice among many — all equal in import. Bishops have the God-given task of teaching in the name of Christ, sanctifying by the power of Christ, and governing with the authority of Christ. "The bishops, as vicars and legates of Christ, govern the particular Churches assigned to them . . . by the authority and sacred power . . . of their Master."[30]

As officials in Christ's Church, the bishops have responsibility for the Church's official public worship, the liturgy. Citing the Second Vatican Council, the *Catechism of the Catholic Church* reminds us that "the bishop is 'the steward of the grace of the supreme priesthood.'"[31] The current liturgical norms approved by the Holy See and the bishops of the United States for the Church in this country are binding on all of the faithful. If priests or lay people set aside liturgical norms, invoking personal preference, they vest themselves with an authority they do not have.

Jesus came to a world of many voices: clamorous, mutually contradictory, contentious, and competing with one another. He arrived to offer us another way, his way. He never said it would be easy. His vision and message would not be accepted by all, would be rejected by some and ignored by others, and would be an occasion of hardship for his disciples. They will "hand you over. . . . You will be hated by all because of my name." This is necessarily so, Jesus went on, because "no disciple is above his teacher, no slave above his master" (see Mt 10:19, 22, 24). But Jesus did tell us that what he brought to us was the truth. "I am the way and the truth and the life" (Jn 14:6).

People today, as always, will be tempted to treat the Church as if it were incidental to salvation, far less important than an individual's subjective feelings and preferences. Perhaps so much attention has been devoted to bishops in recent times because the concept of authority is a "hard saying" in a world where individual freedom and personal interpretation are reckoned to be supreme.

Yet Christ founded his Church to be the gift — objective, identifiable — that leads us to eternal life. We walk away from that gift at our own peril. Given Christ's identification with his Church, which is his body, it is impossible to walk away from the Church without in some way stepping away from Christ.

Who speaks for the Catholic Church? Who speaks for the kingdom? Jesus Christ does, and he wills to do so through the Church's hierarchy.

CHAPTER 12

Politics and the Kingdom

More than a generation ago, a Jesuit priest named Father Robert Drinan made a run for Congress, igniting a firestorm of debate. Secularists wrung their hands, of course, over what they perceived to be a breach of the great wall they wished would separate religion from public life. But others, too, raised concerns. Was it right for a priest to leave aside his ministerial duties and take to the campaign trail — in pursuit of a vocation that properly belongs to the laity? Shouldn't he rather use his ministry of preaching, teaching, and example to lead voters and public officials to do their work in a manner worthy of the Gospels?

The argument played out in the papers. In effect, one side wanted priests to take up direct, partisan political engagement, while the other advocated for the clergy's teaching role.

Both sides were willing to acknowledge that a certain ambiguity would beset the work of a priest-politician. A priest, after all, is a public representative of the Church, an "office-holder" in the kingdom. Wouldn't his status give the appearance of "official" Catholic approval of the policies he advocated as an office-holder in Congress?

I examined the problem in an essay, "Priest, Prophet, and the Political Party," published in the *American Ecclesiastical Review*, a theological journal. For me, these were not merely academic or theoretical questions. They were real-life pastoral concerns.

In those years, I was living in a land far away from my home. I was studying and working in Rome. There, the Christian Democratic Party identified strongly and publicly with the interest of the Catholic Church. In fact, the Christian Democracy movement had arisen in response to the social teachings of the Church and the papal Magisterium. It was founded by devout Catholics who sought to apply the principles of the Gospel to the ordering of society. This action was welcome because the alternative in post-World War II Italy was the insurgent Communist Party, whose totalitarian ideology had already established a reign of terror in the European nations behind the Soviet Union's "Iron Curtain."

Yet, as time went on, the results of this noble ideal of a Christian political party became somewhat confusing. Many voters began to see the relationship not as a partnership between the Church and a political movement, but rather as an identity. To be Catholic was to be a Christian Democrat, and to be a Christian Democrat was to be Catholic. In this confused situation, the terms were interchangeable, and many people viewed the Church as simply an arm of the party. So, if people did not agree with Christian Democracy's policies, they felt they were no longer welcome at church.

I found this sentiment even in families I counted as friends. I asked a man whom I had known for many years why he didn't accompany his wife when she took their children to Mass. He responded: "Why would I? I'm not a Christian Democrat." For him and for many others, religious practice and Christian doctrine had been confused with planks in a party platform — and public policy had been elevated to the status of dogma.

Many clergy were complicit in this. Once I witnessed this at a Mass, when the pastor very forcefully reminded everyone in the congregation that they were morally obliged to vote for the Christian Democratic Party in the upcoming election.

The Christian Democrats may have scored an occasional victory for policies that promoted public morality. But these victories came at a high price. The Church suffered guilt by association whenever a Christian Democrat got caught up in a scandal. The Church was too often identified with a partisan agenda that should have been left to the political process. After all, it is possible to be a devout Catholic and still choose among a range of legitimate political views. Our mission seemed, to many good people, not so much about the Gospel as about partisan politics.

———

We have fared much better in the United States. Here, Catholic pastors have, for the most part, steered a clear course through the troubled waters that result when dealing simultaneously with faith and the call to social responsibility.

The task of the Church's clergy is to proclaim the Gospel and to help the Catholic faithful understand the meaning of Christian doctrine.[32] The translation of the Gospel into the temporal order, on the other hand, is the task of the laity.

The Second Vatican Council encouraged the active participation of the laity in the renewal of the temporal order. The task of the laity is to "build up the Church, sanctify the world and get it to live in Christ." The task "can take on many forms."[33]

Once, in a discussion with a young Catholic politician, I made this distinction between the role of the clergy and the role of the laity, and he replied, "You have the easier part." Easier or harder I'm not sure, but they are different roles.

At the end of 1988, in his letter on the vocation and mission of the laity (*Christifideles Laici*), Blessed John Paul II echoed the question asked by Jesus: "Why do you stand here idle all day?" (Mt 20:6). He went on to explain: "A new state of affairs today, both in the Church and in social, economic, political and cultural life, calls with a particular urgency for the action of the lay faithful."[34]

The task of proclaiming and spreading the faith is particularly challenging today because we live in an age of aggressive secularism. Thus, we may be tempted at times to view our mission as an impossible one. Yet *Christifideles Laici* points out that Jesus never promised that our work would be easy. On the other hand, we know that we have the power of the Holy Spirit to enable us to meet the challenges of the day.

It is not enough to rely on the hierarchy to address serious moral problems in our society. Everyone has to be involved and take an active role. In my twenty-five years as a bishop, I have met with many politicians. They tell me that they hear often from bishops and priests, but not so persistently from the Catholic laity. If that is true, we must change it.

What is it that keeps people silent? Sometimes it's fear. Sometimes it's apathy. Sometimes it's busyness. But sometimes, too, it's an overriding political allegiance. Years ago I was working with a number of Catholic parishes as they consolidated schools to try to cut costs and keep tuition affordable. A local activist was infuriated by our efforts and demanded to know why all the schools would not be kept open. Someone suggested she might want to direct her question to the politicians who did not support school choice legislation. That, however, was taboo. She responded, "Oh, no! I belong to that party."

The voice and engagement of the laity will ultimately determine the direction of our society. The voice of Catholic physicians needs to be heard, loud and clear, in the area of health care. Catholic lawyers need to speak out on the administration of justice and our constitutionally protected liberties. Catholic parents and teachers should be involved in educational issues. Catholic universities and colleges should be in the forefront articulating Catholic principles and providing the intellectual and academic support that allows people to give an account of their faith.

Pope John Paul said it well: "It is necessary, then, to keep a watchful eye on this our world, with its problems and values, its unrest and hopes, its defeats and triumphs: a world whose economic, social, political, and cultural affairs pose problems and grave difficulties."[35]

He described the participation of the lay faithful in the life of the Church as "communion." He began with the scriptural image of the branches and the vine: "I am the true vine and my Father is the vine grower. . . . Remain in me, as I remain in you" (Jn 15:1, 4). Here we learn that, precisely because he or she is an important part of the Church, each individual layperson is called to carry out the mission and work of the *whole* Church. That's solidarity. That's subsidiarity at work.

Every baptized person is configured to Christ as a member of his body, and every ordained priest and bishop is configured to Christ as head of that body. Together they bring the new Body of Christ to fullness as it makes its way through time and history.

From time to time, some Catholics speak out in disagreement with this or that moral teaching of the Church, usually in the area of sexual morality, but sometimes also on issues dealing with care for the poor, protection of human life, or the treatment of immigrants. Whatever the issue, the media tend to portray these views as *proof* that the leadership of the Church is out of touch with contemporary thinking. When confronted with the fact that there are some Catholics who do not fully understand or accept Church teaching, I respond that I need to do a better job of teaching. Faith and morals don't change according to polls. Sometimes all of us just need to do a better job of teaching and listening. This includes the lay faithful, who must be part of the voice of the Church, and who have a critically important role to play in spreading the Gospel.

———

To be Catholic is to admit of a wide range of opinions and methods. There is no Catholic position on the management of public utilities. Devout Catholics may hold an almost infinite variety of opinions on taxation.

We must observe a clear distinction between dogmas of the faith, such as the resurrection of Jesus and the assumption of the Blessed Mother into heaven, and those moral principles proclaimed by the Church that are rooted in creation and written on the human heart as the natural moral law. We do not ask the state to impose or even recognize our dogmas. The principle of the free exercise of religion clearly prohibits the state from doing this. But that principle does *not* prevent us from advocating the recognition of universal moral principles — accessible by reason alone — as a valid rationale for public policy and as the norm against which such policy should be measured.

Laws require a point of reference. Every law assumes the existence of right and wrong and prescribes behavior accordingly. Every law is cast in terms of "ought": you ought to do this, and ought not to do that. Thus every law is implicitly and unavoidably moral. Life does not and cannot unfold in a moral vacuum. Human beings have a moral north star that guides our moral compass. There is a moral order built into God's creation and into human nature. Just as there are physical laws that are a part of the created order — the law of gravity, for example — so there is also in humanity a law that leads us to admire moral goods such as justice, courage, and temperance. Philosophers for millennia have recognized it.

Deep within our heart and conscience is the recognition, for example, that you must not kill others, just as you do not want others to feel free to kill you. The injunction "You shall not kill" — rooted in our human nature, proclaimed by our conscience, and confirmed in God's revelation — applies to all innocent human life.

In a democracy, every citizen must accept some responsibility for the direction of the country. When we vote, we may not check our integrity at the door of the polling place. We need to bring our moral values and vision to the process. Otherwise public policy would soon have no moral coherence — and no moral authority.

Integrity requires the same consistency in elected or appointed officials. If one has been chosen for a job, it should be assumed that both vote and behavior will follow on one's conscience. Citizens vote for *persons* whom they believe will exercise good judgment and prudence, and will follow their conscience.

Every member of the faithful, especially those engaged in political activity, must act out of a *well-formed* Christian conscience. Lawmakers have to consider the moral implications of their votes. Aristotle pointed out many centuries ago: the law is a teacher. For many people, what is legal becomes what is right. It should be, but it is not always so. Slavery is one historical example. Abortion is a current one. We live in a culture now that has been formed by laws that permit the casual destruction of the most innocent and most vulnerable human lives. What do such laws teach? What sort of culture are they forming?

It is the job of the bishops to make clear how the Gospel message applies to the circumstances of our day. But it is the task of the laity to make an effort to understand those teachings — especially those that are most relevant to their work — and apply them to the practical order of public policy.

It is for this reason that the bishops have so consistently taught that abortion, which takes the life of an unborn human being, is intrinsically evil. It can never be justified. Abortion is an action clearly and decisively condemned in the teaching of the early Church. The first-century document known as the *Didache*, or "Teaching of the Twelve Apostles," addresses abortion in terms that evoke the Ten Commandments: "Thou shalt not procure an abortion, nor destroy a newborn child." The Letter of Barnabas, composed just slightly later, treats the matter in the same way: "Thou shalt not slay the child by procuring abortion." The teaching is echoed in the following years by Christians throughout the Roman world: Athenagoras in Greece, Tertullian in North Africa, Minucius Felix in Italy.

Certainly no position has been so clearly and strongly stated by the bishops of the United States. It is as clear today as it has always been: the Catholic Church opposes abortion because abortion is a moral evil.

As abortion is wrong, so — quite logically — legislative support for abortion is wrong. The Vatican Congregation for the Doctrine of the Faith, citing the teaching of Blessed John Paul II, recently clarified that voting for legislation supporting abortion is gravely wrong.[36]

So often the attempt to justify voting for pro-abortion legislation is made by the claim that the legislator, personally, is opposed to abortion but wants to allow people a choice. The flaw in this argument is obvious. When you choose, you choose something. When you say "I choose," you have to complete the sentence. As Pope John Paul II reminded us, ours is a choice "between the 'culture of life' and the 'culture of death.'"[37]

No one would take seriously the claim of a legislator that he or she is personally opposed to child pornography but feels that it really should be left to the choice of the individual. We don't even do that with smoking in most public places.

Support for abortion is in a category far beyond other politically driven decisions, such as the rate of taxation or the advisability of a new bond issue. There is no natural moral law written in the hearts of all people regarding public funding of a new transit system or about a new sales tax. But there is about killing innocent human life.

All of us have an obligation to be informed on how critical the life-and-death issue of abortion is, and how profoundly and intrinsically evil is the destruction of unborn human life. If our nation was founded upon the "laws of nature and nature's God," then abortion renders null the most fundamental right hallowed by America's founders: the right to life.

The legality of abortion has enabled the widespread use of other technologies that routinely involve the destruction of pre-born life: embryonic stem-cell research, for example; contraceptives that are abortifacient; and *in vitro* fertilization. For obvious reasons, the Church condemns these practices as well.

———

In November 2007, the bishops of the United States issued a call to political responsibility titled *Forming Consciences for Faithful Citizenship*. Subsequently, the bishops' conference reaffirmed the value of this document as a clear statement of the principles of Catholic teaching that must be applied by individual Catholics to the issues of the day. Catholic faithful can find guidance here when addressing the arduous task of applying the teaching of the Church to practical political positions.

The statement begins by calling our attention to the constant teaching of the Church that Christians should play their full role as citizens: "In the Catholic Tradition, responsible citizenship is a virtue, and participation in political life is a moral obligation . . . The Catholic call to faithful citizenship affirms the importance of political participation and insists that public service is a worthy vocation."

In a democracy where each of us has a voice and vote, we assume responsibility for the direction our country takes in matters that have clear moral content. We are not free to stand back and allow morally objectionable activities to transpire under the protection of the law as if legality somehow conferred morality on our activities as a people, a society, a nation.

Every citizen can and should participate in political life. For a layperson, this can take the form of voting, actively supporting a political party or specific candidate, or running for and holding public office.

Forming Consciences reminds us that we bring important assets to the political dialogue about our nation's future: "We bring a consistent moral framework — drawn from basic human reason that is illuminated by Scripture and the teaching of the Church — for assessing issues, political platforms, and campaigns."

We as Catholics bring a God-given gift: the message of the Gospel — the vision that Jesus shares. Our faith in God's word and our recognition of a natural moral law should make us prodigies of political participation.

The faithful should fulfill their civic duties guided by a Christian conscience, and thus *every Catholic has an obligation to properly form his or her conscience*. This requires lifelong effort, and it's not optional. The bishops, for their part, have a duty to accommodate those efforts, and so must preach and teach with clarity and constancy.

Nevertheless, the translation of moral imperatives into political action and public policy remains the work of the laity.

———

One of the primary tasks of the laity is the conversion of the temporal order, so that our public policy is guided by divine law. In his encyclical *Deus Caritas Est*, Pope Benedict XVI wrote that "the direct duty to work for a just ordering of society . . . is proper to the lay faithful. As citizens of the State, they are called to take part in public life in a personal capacity."[38] This duty is more critical than ever in today's political environment, where Catholics may feel politically disenfranchised, especially because there may not be a political party or candidate that fully reflects the range of Catholic social and moral teaching, particularly on the issues that claim priority in our decision-making process. The United States Conference of Catholic Bishops' document points out "this is not a time for retreat or discouragement; rather, it is a time for renewed engagement."

A conscientious Catholic seeks to hear the life-giving words of Jesus Christ, to know their meaning, and also to live them honestly and with integrity. While our conscience is our guide, we need to form it with the words of truth and life.

Once we have formed it, we will be compelled to act. Only if we act — and act rightly — will we realize, will we manifest, the kingdom coming to be now and see its fullness in the life to come.

CHAPTER 13

The Kingdom's Healing Power

My high regard for doctors began at an early age. I still remember the visit of our family doctor to our house. He was there to check on my brother, who had a sore throat. I decided I had one, too, since it seemed likely to guarantee a day off from school. A bond that lasted fifty years began when the doctor announced to my mother that I, too, should stay home that day but that, unlike my brother, I would certainly be well enough "to go to school tomorrow." He remained my doctor until he died at ninety-one. Every year, I visited him for my annual checkup, which later included words of encouragement for my ministry, as well as advice for my health.

The Church indeed blesses physicians, for in the world they are the image of Christ the Healer. When Jesus listed signs of the kingdom, many of them were cures of physical ailments: "the blind regain their sight, the lame walk, lepers are cleansed, the deaf hear, the dead are raised" (Mt 11:5).

The early Church took up Jesus' healing ministry. There is evidence of miraculous cures from the age of the apostles onward. But *most* of the Church's healing took place in a more ordinary way, through the practice of medicine.

Indeed, it can be argued that widespread institutionalized health care arose, for the most part, within and around the Catholic Church. In the fourth century, St. Basil the Great built a network of social-welfare ministries in the city of Caesarea in Cappadocia (modern Turkey). It included hospitals and hospices, as well as trade schools where people with disabilities could learn professional skills. The campus grew so vast that the locals named it the "New City." We know that a friend of Basil, St. Caesarius, practiced medicine and even served as personal physician to the emperor.

Before Christianity, the practice of medicine had been erratic at best. Four centuries before Christ, Hippocrates set down an ethical code for physicians, but there is no evidence that it was observed in most of the world. Practitioners like Galen (in the second and third centuries after Christ) gathered the inherited wisdom on physiology and surgery and worked it out in a theoretical framework, but the services of such men were available only to the wealthiest citizens. For others, "healing" was offered at the pagan temples of the god Asclepius, but it consisted mostly of rituals. A sick person might spend the night sleeping in the Asclepian sanctuary and in the morning report his dreams for priestly interpretation. His prescription would then be based on the content of his dreams.

With the growth of the Church, we find something new in the field of medicine — the intersection of experimental science with the practice of charity. We find the beginnings of true health *care*. The early monasteries of the Egyptian desert considered this to be one of many ways they reflected Christ to the world. The monks combed the medical textbooks of their day and compiled their own guides to pharmacology. In recent years, the U.S. pharmaceutical industry has funded research at Ivy League universities into these ancient prescriptions to determine what we moderns might learn from those ancient monks.

But the *care* is what made the greatest difference — and the care is the most valuable thing a Catholic can put into the practice of medicine. One of the most moving stories from the ancient Church is the account in Eusebius's *Church History* of a great epidemic that struck the Roman Empire in the early third century, and how Christians remained with the afflicted as everyone else abandoned the city.

Even the eminent physician Galen fled the site of epidemics. In those days before antibiotics, he knew he couldn't do anything to stop a communicable disease. Most people, in fact, abandoned their sick family members in order to save themselves and those who had not yet contracted the disease.

Many Christians, however, felt compelled to *stay* with the sick, feed them, wash them, clothe them, and pray with them. Modern studies have shown that patients who receive such minimal "comfort care" are much more likely to survive than those who are left alone. Christians knew that whatever they did for the sick, they did for Christ (see Mt 25:35-40), so they did whatever they could. They did it not only for their co-religionists, but for non-Christians as well. Surely many of those pagans who survived — thanks to Christian care — came eventually to recognize the power of Christ the Healer, *Christus Medicus*, Christ the Doctor.

This is the spirit that has animated Catholic health care and medical research, from the lifetime of the evangelist St. Luke (who tradition tells us was a physician), through the work of the desert monks, down to the scientific discoveries of giants like the priest Gregor Mendel and the Catholic layman Louis Pasteur.

The Catholic Church is involved in health care because Catholics believe that care of the sick is an important part of Christ's command to serve. The Gospels reveal Jesus as a healer. In Matthew's Gospel, Jesus touches a man and "his leprosy was cleansed" (Mt 8:3). In Mark, Jesus restores a man's sight (Mk 10:49-52). In Luke, he heals the woman with a hemorrhage (Lk 8:43-44). In John, he cures a man who had been paralyzed for thirty-eight years (Jn 5:1-9).

For a Catholic in the healing professions, medicine is more than a job, more than a necessary task. It is God's mercy and love at work among us and in us, through human hands, words, actions, and hearts.

There is however still more. We are convinced that sickness, pain, suffering, and death are a part of God's providential plan. We believe that suffering is a mystery that is unfathomable, but not impenetrable, because God has shared our life in Christ, and Christ's life culminated in suffering and death that led to his resurrection and glory.

A true follower of Christ helps others to understand God's plan, live it, and experience the redemptive dimension of human suffering. For the Catholic, illness and death take on a positive and distinctive meaning when understood in the context of the redemptive power of Jesus' suffering and death.

Jesus himself said: "If anyone wishes to come after me, he must deny himself and take up his cross daily and follow me" (Lk 9:23). His cross was like an altar, where he offered his life as a sacrifice for the sake of others. We too can offer our own "cross" of suffering this way. St. Paul wrote to the Colossians: "Now I rejoice in my sufferings for your sake, and in my flesh I am filling up what is lacking in the afflictions of Christ on behalf of his body, which is the Church" (Col 1:24). What was "lacking" in Christ's suffering? Only the portion he left for us to share, so that we could share *all* his life, so that we could face death with his strength, and so that we could one day share his resurrection.

The Catholic attitude is not weary resignation to the inevitable. It is a way to triumph, to victory. It is a royal way, because it has been traversed by our King.

For a Catholic, there is a mysterious *sense* to suffering, a sense that brings serenity, meaning, and purpose — even to pain, and even to death.

———

When we look to the "how" of Catholic health care, we realize that it is not just an institutional resolve to care for the sick, but also a *personal* commitment to provide it in a specific way, within a particular context, according to a unique vision of human life — a vision revealed in the person of Jesus Christ. Faith provides not only our motivation for getting involved in the first place, but also the direction our involvement should take. Faith points the way we should approach the options technology offers us today.

Catholic health care providers, like all providers, value efficiency and cost-effectiveness, but never at the expense of principle. We can identify several fundamental principles underlying Catholic care: a profound respect for the transcendent value of the human person; the recognition that human life is a gift from God; the notion that we are stewards of that life and not its arbiters; and, that the purpose of health-care ministry is to help human life flourish.

Care for the sick recognizes also that, eventually, all physical remedies fail. In the cycle of life it begins, grows, matures, declines, and ends in death. Catholic health care takes place in the wider perspective that all life, even when medicine can do no more, is still sacred as it seeks its ultimate perfection in eternal life with God.

Once, when called to anoint an elderly parishioner who had been failing for many years, I was greeted by one of her adult children with the caution that I should not let the mother know that she was seriously failing. I am not sure what she thought her mother would think about my being there to administer the sacrament at that late hour in the evening if she wasn't "seriously failing." When I greeted her and asked was she ready to receive the sacrament, she said with a faint but real smile, "Yes, Father, but you will have to help my children understand that I am dying. God is calling me home."

———

Catholic health care institutions, as a part of their mission, bear witness within the profession and within the wider community, to the worth of human life. Catholic health care also gives public witness that modern medicine, with all its technological possibilities, must be guided by the moral law. We are not free to do whatever we can; but as rational, reflective persons we are required to do what we ought.

Thus we prohibit some procedures because they would actually undermine our attempts to achieve some human good.

The first-century Christian document called the *Didache* begins with the line, "There are two ways, one of life and one of death, but a great difference between the two ways." That statement is no less true and no less urgent today.

In our society, there are two ways — two approaches to ethical and moral decisions. One is a way that marks out God's plan and respects the preservation and enrichment of human life within that plan. The other way emphasizes the autonomy of the human person, who is assumed to have limitless freedom to manipulate and reorder the human body. Blessed John Paul II, in his encyclical letter *The Gospel of Life*, describes the divergence of these views as a struggle between the "culture of death" and the "civilization of love."

Nowhere, perhaps, is the traditional view of life, death, and God's sovereignty more seriously challenged than in the medical field, where technological and scientific advances often outpace the necessary moral reflection. More and more, we meet professionals who have concluded that moral reflection is unnecessary and superfluous.

How can that be when we are talking about such matters as physician-assisted suicide, organ harvesting and donation, reproductive technology, cloning, and behavior modification through medication. These matters, not long ago, were the stuff of science fiction. Today they're covered under many insurance plans. What is disturbing is the call from some politicians and government bureaucrats that all health care plans must provide for some of these procedures, perhaps eventually all of them. Even more distressing is the roughshod rejection of religious freedom and freedom of conscience as these policies are imposed.

In a recent interview I was asked what I considered the major ethical challenge facing Catholic health care today. My reply then, which I continue to consider valid, was the erosion of our freedom of conscience and our freedom of religious liberty as we continue to engage in Catholic health care services. We will experience increased political pressures to accept as legitimate health care procedures sterilization, abortion, and sex-assignment surgery, to mention just a few.

I remain convinced that the government should not be defining what constitutes health care and what specific medical procedures must be used.

Catholic institutions need to be free to say there are some actions that they cannot do and will not do. Given the long history of Catholic health care in our nation and its huge contribution to indigent care, we must not give in on the long-standing principle of our democratic and pluralistic society that we carry out our ministry in accord with our conscience.

It is our faith that compels us to care for "the least of these," and it is that same faith that requires us to say "no" to those things which threaten human life and dignity.

The Church has a duty and a right to speak out in defense of the natural moral order and for the universal right to adequate health care. Only religion can sustain those values that make possible a lasting *common good* — which is more than temporary political expediency. Without such a value system, there is a very real danger that human choices will be motivated solely by convenience and profit.

Given the importance of Catholic health care ministry, we recognize the need to confront, with imagination and courage, the market forces that drive the health-care industry today. Without energetic and united cooperation, we can quickly and very easily find ourselves marginalized in an area of the human endeavor that has always been an important part of Christian mission and ministry.

Technology and science can empower us to do many wonderful things. They have, for example, extended life expectancy far beyond the dreams of even a generation ago. But what human technology and science cannot answer is: *Ought we to do everything we can?*

The play *A Man for All Seasons* dramatizes the conflict between Sir Thomas More and King Henry VIII. One scene depicts an exchange between More and Thomas Cromwell, who replaced More as chancellor of England. Quite unlike More, Cromwell does the king's bidding, regardless of what he bids. St. Thomas More advises him that this is a grave mistake: "Your task as counselor to the king," More says, "is not to tell him what he can do; this he already knows. Your obligation is to tell him what he ought to do."

———

Catholic health care is an expression of the healing ministry of the Lord, and so it is part of the mission Jesus left to the Church. Precisely because it is a ministry and not a business, Catholic health care — like every other ministry in the Church — engages not only the oversight of doctors and administrative executives, but also the bishop's pastoral governance.

Collaboration and communication between Catholic health care providers and the bishops are necessary as we sustain the mission and identity of Catholic health care services.

There is a place where the bishop representing the Church as a whole relates to the hospital or health care system which is a part of the Church. For a college or university, the entity's mission statement provides the point of intersection. For Catholic health care institutions, the *Ethical and Religious Directives for Catholic Health Care Services* (now in its fifth edition) provides the forum for this convergence.

Now that Catholic health care providers are moving into a new governance model, it is important that, in order to ensure Catholic identity, the bishops are not left out of the picture.

Those who work in the field of medicine have an exalted vocation. They didn't pick a career. They were called to do the work of Christ the Healer — which is a crucial dimension of the reign of Christ the King. Every action of their every day presents them with a decision. It is the choice of "two ways" the Church presented in the first century. Those who choose the "way of life" will help people live life better. They will also help prepare people for death, when that time comes — yet true *care* makes even dying a way to life.

In the world: again, it's the kingdom.

CHAPTER 14

Education for the Kingdom

"You will know the truth, and the truth will set you free"
(Jn 8:32).

Christianity has always placed a premium on knowledge. Integral to our salvation is receiving "the truth" and knowing it. Jesus' disciples called him "Teacher" (in Hebrew, *Rabbi*), and when he sent the disciples forth in his name, he made "teaching" an indispensable part of their mission (Mt 28:20). So teaching would forever be a sign of the kingdom. In the Catholic Church, teachers would forever serve as images of Christ the Teacher.

In the letters of St. Paul we find that teachers were prominent members of the early Church (1 Cor 12:28), ranked with prophets, evangelists, and pastors (Eph 4:11). Paul saw himself as a teacher (2 Tm 1:11) after the model of his master.

Jesus "taught the crowds" (Lk 5:3). "He taught them as one having authority" (Mt 7:29). He taught in the Temple (Jn 7:14) and in the synagogues (Lk 4:15); he taught in the streets (Lk 13:26); he taught from a boat (Mk 4:1-2).

Jesus was "the Teacher," and so he taught. Then, at the end of his earthly ministry, he passed his teaching ministry on to the Church, and so the Church teaches. We catechize in parish religious-education classes. We organize schools to teach the truth. We build colleges, pre-schools, graduate schools, elementary schools, high schools, and seminaries. We sponsor continuing-education courses. We offer seminars to train our people for liturgical ministry. Catholic parents teach their children from the moment of birth, acting as their "primary educators," according to the Church.[39] Catholics share Christ's ministry, and so we are teachers. We teach.

The Catholic Church has a well-earned reputation for teaching. The secular university system, as we know it today, is actually a product of the medieval Church, which established its schools (for example, the University of Paris) to train theologians and clergy.

It is a blessing, then, to be Catholic and American. For our country, like our Church, prizes education. Compulsory school attendance has been the law of the land — in all fifty states — for almost a hundred years. The Church in this country built a vast system of Catholic education. We enjoyed the freedom to do so.

As Catholics and as Americans we place a premium value on education. Perhaps it is our country's Christian "upbringing" that has trained its citizens to associate knowledge with freedom. "You will know the truth, and the truth will set you free." In America, education has provided a greater number of people with a greater freedom of opportunity. In the Old World, certain pursuits — scholarship, for example — were reserved almost exclusively for the aristocracy. In America, academic degrees have been open to anyone who wished to work hard at studies and scrape together the tuition. Indeed, in the Land of the Free, we expect education to be a part of almost any rags-to-riches story.

Education for the kingdom brings with it the unique kind of freedom that Jesus reveals. He intended his Gospel, his revelation, his truth, to set us free from errors about our own identity . . . to set us free from bondage to sin . . . and to set us free from the sentence of spiritual and physical death. Jesus reveals to us who God is and who, therefore, we are. He teaches us that we are all created by a loving God who calls us to share by adoption in his own divine life. When we work as Catholic educators, we share in the mission of Jesus, our king, and in the name of his kingdom, which we find in the Church. So we educate people not just for exams, but for life eternal. We educate the whole person: mind, body, and spirit.

———

We provide that teaching — the revelation, the introduction to Christ — at every level. A Catholic who teaches very small children must reflect Christ's love and discipline. A Catholic who teaches high-school students must serve as a model of integrity, provoking serious thought at one of the most important stages in the formation of conscience.

The higher the level of education, the more challenging is the educator's role. The popes have, in recent years, devoted much attention to the renewal of Catholic education at the highest levels: colleges and universities. Since this is where other future teachers are trained, the renewal should have far-reaching effects in educational ministry.

Blessed John Paul II set the agenda for this renewal in his apostolic constitution on Catholic universities, *Ex Corde Ecclesiae*. There he reminded all of us that the university itself, as an institution, was "born from the heart of the Church."

In the vision of the kingdom of God being introduced, manifested, and realized in this world, the university exists by a special calling from God. "By vocation," Pope John Paul II continued, the university with its professors and scholars "is dedicated to research, to teaching and to education of students who freely associate with their teachers in a common love of knowledge."

Those words have a modern ring to them, but the Holy Father was actually quoting from a letter Pope Alexander IV wrote to the University of Paris in 1255!

In the United States, Catholic colleges and universities were born from the desire to provide a distinctive sort of education, academically excellent, and marked by the special character of Catholic doctrine, tradition, and world view. Catholic identity would be reflected not only in the classroom, but also in campus life. Theology would be given an honored place in the curriculum, supreme among the sciences. The Church's liturgy would serve as the deepest source of the campus's spiritual vitality, intellectual energy, and familial unity. The bishop would guide the university's spiritual, ecclesial mission as he guides all ministries in the Church.

These are signs of Catholic identity, and so they are signs of the kingdom. Hallmarks — distinguishing signs — are necessary if the phrase "Catholic education" is to have meaning. A Catholic university should be an academic center where the faith permeates the culture. The liturgical celebration of the faith should be an integral part of the school's program and routine. The institution's communion with the Church should be clearly seen in how the university relates to the bishop as head of the local Church.

Today, however, there is an additional "sign" that we need to highlight. A Catholic college or university should reflect its identity by engaging the issues and questions challenging our culture and society, and doing it in an intellectually consistent, socially responsible, and thoroughly Catholic way.

Our institutions have an advantage here. A Catholic university has the unique capacity to deal with and emphasize the spiritual dimension of human life. Revelation, religious conviction, and faith enable the student and professor to carry our understanding of human existence beyond the natural and physically verifiable and into the spiritual dimension needed for a full human life.

Among the benefits of a Catholic college or university is its ability to act as a bridge between the wider community and the Church. As young people grow, their faith must be part of their engagement of the world around them. On a Catholic campus, the faith should be woven into the entire fabric of university life. That is the only way the university can help the student engage the culture from a uniquely Catholic perspective.

Not only students benefit from this. The university's local community does. The Church does. The students' future employers and spouses do. So does the wider *academic* community. Catholic universities, when they are true to their name and their heritage, contribute a distinctive voice to the great conversations taking place in the fields of scholarship and research. The academic world, by its nature, celebrates diversity and freedom. Thus, we will offer our most valuable contribution when we are working in a way that's most faithful to our own distinct identity. It is essential that our voice be true to who we are.

The challenge and invitation to seek first the kingdom of God is not directed solely to individuals, to disciples, to believers, but also and inevitably to the institutional expressions of the Church's life and mission. In this light we see the special role of those who administer and teach in colleges and universities that rejoice in their Catholic identity and their participation in the noble calling to impart the message "to seek first the kingdom of God."

———

Universities, too, must pass tests, ensuring that their curricula and research meet the standards of the various fields of study. In every area of academic endeavor, accrediting agencies set the standards, monitor the schools, and enforce compliance.

Just as biology professors must have proper certification, so must theology professors. A theologian must possess a *mandatum* from the local bishop. The *mandatum* is the credential that affirms, in a verifiable manner, that the Catholic professor who teaches the Church's sciences does so in communion with the Church.

Processes of accreditation are a standard part of academic life, in every field, in every department, in every program and discipline. What is taught in the classroom must reflect the theory and practice that's current in the wider world. Law schools must keep current with court decisions and appeals processes. Medical schools must keep up with advances in technology and pharmacology as well as the demands of the federal regulatory agencies. To fall behind in these areas would render a school's curriculum substandard — and its students ineligible for certain grants, aid, and other privileges. The accrediting agency has the authority to ensure that a school practices truth in advertising: if we call someone a professor of engineering, then that person should profess engineering as it is practiced and as it is defined by those who hold authentic authority in the matter.

A Catholic university endeavors to teach, among other things, the faith of the Church and to advance that faith by a more profound understanding of its implications and applications in our day. So the university necessarily must relate to the rest of the Church and especially to its pastors, the bishops.

The Church's articulation of Catholic doctrine is traditionally called the Magisterium. Its very name comes from the Latin term for teaching office. The Magisterium represents the Church's exercise of the responsibility, assigned by Christ to the apostles and their successors, the bishops, for the care and interpretation of divine revelation. The Magisterium accredits or affirms that what is taught as Catholic is recognizable as Catholic.

———

Since theology has divine revelation as its starting point, theological science is different from every other type of science. Intrinsic to theology is both the objective truth of revelation and the normative guidance of the Magisterium, or teaching office within the Church.

Thus, in the Church's understanding of academic freedom, the propositions of theologians do not automatically translate into authentic Church teaching. Involved in the wider process is the recognition of the role of the Holy Spirit, which manifests itself in the "sense of the faith" discernible in the Church as a whole and in the approval of the bishops.

In the Catholic model, the whole Church participates in the process of the development of doctrine, but each part of the Church participates according to its own gifts and ministries. Theologians are free to speculate. They may argue in favor of their theological positions; but the final judgment of these positions belongs to the Catholic bishops, who have received from Jesus the power of "binding and loosing" (Mt 16:19 and 18:18).

On the major issues of our doctrinal and moral lives, there cannot exist alternate or opposing truths. To claim otherwise is to threaten the very unity of the faith — unity throughout the world and unity through all time. The Church certainly observes a historical process of doctrinal development, but this does not mean that the doctrine of one generation can flatly contradict the doctrine of another generation. Ultimate responsibility for judging genuine development rests with the bishops who succeed the college of apostles.

Sometimes it is proposed, in defense of those who dissent from Church teaching or who do not present the full content of the Church's teaching, that they are really "heroes" of conscience. There is much more, however, to being a true hero of conscience than simply continuing to adhere to one's personal opinion despite correction.

The Church has always understood that individual conscience is not self-sufficient. It needs to be educated. The *Catechism of the Catholic Church* explains that the "education of conscience is indispensable for human beings who are subjected to negative influences and tempted by sin to prefer their own judgment and to reject authoritative teachings."[40] Conscience is a rational judgment that, like any judgment, must be informed and weighed. It is not simply a personal conviction that gainsays any standard of right and wrong. It is part of the Church's mandate from Christ, and an essential part of the bishop's vocation in the Church, to help us make those rational judgments of conscience with the aid of Scripture and tradition.

Everyone, therefore, has a moral duty to see to it that his or her conscience is informed. While true in matters of moral decision-making, this is all the more crucial in matters of faith. The Catholic faith is founded upon divine revelation and contains truths that exceed human understanding and must be accepted on the basis of the divine authority. According to Catholic teaching, bishops as successors of the apostles are the authoritative teachers of the truths of faith. Individual judgment or opinion based on human reason, no matter how sincerely held, can never have the last word.

If one denies, even in good conscience, an authoritative teaching of the Church, as proposed by its highest teaching authority, one has weakened the bond with the Church and is no longer able to claim the privilege to minister within and on behalf of the Church. At issue is not one's freedom of conscience. Rather it is a question of rejecting Church teaching and, at the same time, wishing to continue to speak as a representative of the Church.

To call any school "Catholic" is to label it as an intellectual and academic partner of the Church. To call a school "Catholic" is to make a serious commitment: that the things that happen on campus will align with the Gospel as it has been proclaimed by the Church through two millennia.

A Catholic school should function as an outpost of the kingdom, a place where the faith is taught and "caught," a place where the Gospel is transmitted by modeling, by mentoring, by lectures, by libraries, and by means of technology. When Catholics teach this way, they are teaching like their Master, who taught only the truth, taught in every venue he could, and taught almost without ceasing. When he took breaks, it should be noted, it was in order to pray.

His task was urgent, and so is ours. Like him, we are educating people to live in the kingdom. Our work as educators at every level is to help those who look to us for knowledge, wisdom, and counsel "to seek first the kingdom."

CHAPTER 15

The Priesthood: Witness of the Kingdom

Entering, I found the usual hush of a sickroom. Gathered around the bed were family members and friends. The man at the center of the scene was a friend and brother priest.

His cancer was in its final stages, and he was clearly preparing himself for the great journey ahead. I was there to do what priests do: to give a sick person sacramental anointing.

I prayed the ritual prayers and anointed his forehead. When it came to the point in the sacrament when I would ordinarily have anointed his hands, he turned them over, palm down, as a simple reminder that his hands had already, once and irrevocably, been anointed. He had been permanently consecrated to Christ on the day of his ordination.

In the ancient kingdom of Israel, who was anointed? Priests, prophets, and kings were. It was the ritual prerequisite for their task.

In the kingdom of God, Christ is not only king; he is also high priest. In his Church on earth, he exercises this office through those he has called to share in his priesthood — those who have received the Sacrament of Holy Orders.

From the moment of his ordination, the Catholic priest is himself a sign of the kingdom. He serves the kingdom as it emerges on earth, in and through the ministry of the Church. At the same time, he is a *sign of the kingdom* as it will be in glory, at the consummation of history. Jesus himself willed priests to witness to the kingdom in this way (see Mt 22:30 and 19:12). The apostles in turn, wherever they went, faithfully appointed priests, and then provided for the same to be done in the future. Paul begins his Letter to Titus with that instruction (see Ti 1:5). The Church ordained these men by the "laying on of hands" (see Acts 13:3).

The word "priest" comes from the Greek *presbyteros*, meaning "elder." In the New Testament and still today, a man might be ordained to this office when quite young. Nevertheless, in the Church, our supernatural society, a priest serves as an elder serves in a natural society. He teaches, and he leads in a fatherly way. We do not hesitate to address him as "Father."

———

When Jesus was preparing his disciples for the day when he would no longer be with them, he called them to the foundational element of discipleship: faith.

He said to Peter: "Who do you say that I am?" (see Mt 16:13-17).

Peter replied, "You are the Messiah, the Son of the living God."

That is an act of faith, as Jesus himself makes clear: "Blessed are you, Simon, son of Jonah. For flesh and blood has not revealed this to you, but my heavenly Father." Peter had drawn this creed not from human testimony, but by God's grace. Furthermore, he trusted God's word. He spoke out of an active faith.

The priesthood, however, is still more than this. It is more than an act of faith. It is a commitment to ministry — a commitment to service.

Ministry, service: the words in their original languages (both Greek and Hebrew) had a dual meaning that they preserve in English. They mean hard labor (as in the "service industries"), but they also mean ritual worship (as in "church services"). Both senses apply to the priesthood of Jesus Christ, who was an exalted priest-king like Melchizedek (see Heb 5:10), yet who took "the form of a slave" and "humbled himself, becoming obedient" (Phil 2:7-8). Both senses apply to the Catholic priests who share in Christ's ministry.

Peter made his act of faith, but Our Lord would call him to something more. In the days after his resurrection, Jesus once again encountered Peter and challenged him, this time not about his faith but about his commitment to ministry. He said: "Simon, son of John, do you love me more than these?"

Simon Peter replied, "Yes, Lord, you know that I love you."

Jesus simply rejoined, "Feed my sheep."

Again a second and a third time, Jesus continued the interrogation: "Do you love me more than these?" The answer was the same, "Yes," and the rejoinder identical: "Then feed my sheep."

This is the heart of Peter's ministry — and the ministry of any Catholic priest. To love Christ is to tend his flock.

———

Salvation comes by way of baptism. Everyone who is baptized is incorporated into Christ. Baptism is not only a pledge that Christ will someday return in glory. It is also the means by which the present-day Body of Christ — the Church, the kingdom — becomes the very power of Christ working in our world.

To serve this community of the elect, Jesus set aside those who would devote their labors to the tasks shared by all the baptized, but also to the specific task of serving the whole

Body of Christ. Through the Sacrament of Holy Orders, men are specially conformed to Christ, empowered to serve his people as ministers of divine grace.

Holy orders takes its place as the second great differentiation within the Church of Christ. Those whom we call "priests" are ordained by God to participate more specifically in the priesthood of Christ, to serve the community through specifically ministerial, priestly, sacramental works.

Yet this "setting apart" or "differentiation" is not meant to divide or establish a class system within the kingdom. It is meant to facilitate the life and function of the Body. The priest is no more separated from lay people than lay people are separated from the world in which they live. The common priesthood of the faithful, conferred in baptism, is interrelated with the ministerial priesthood because each in its own way is a participation in the one priesthood of Christ, and each is unintelligible without the other. Priests are not somehow "more saved" than lay people; but they are called to a more complete and explicit dedication to the task of sanctification.

Christ's work was to initiate the kingdom. The Church is to complete that task. The believer, by virtue of baptism, becomes a member of the Church and is empowered to be an apostle of Christ . . . to the world. The priest, by virtue of ordination, is configured to Christ in a unique way to facilitate the holiness of the whole Church. The priest is empowered to nourish, mold, and direct the priestly people in their common goal of bringing about the new creation.

The priest, therefore, has a unique relationship to the Church. He has a particular role in the Church because of his vocation and ordination. He has been called to serve the people of God in a specific manner. He has been charged and empowered to build up the entire Body of Christ. In this sense, he is the power of Christ in glory manifesting itself in the

Body of Christ in time. The purpose of this power is the goal of Christ himself — to energize and help realize his kingdom in time and space.

———

A priest shares in the bishop's threefold ministry: to teach, to govern, and to sanctify.

To Teach. The first task of the priest is to teach and preach the Gospel. The priest must testify not only to the person of Jesus, but to the content of his revelation. As a witness to the content of the faith, his principal characteristics are two: to proclaim it in its entirety and to testify to it as it is received.

Through the preaching of our clergy, the truth of God breaks into this world. This truth is what makes us free — what makes us whole — what gives us life. To know Christ is to know God and to live forever. The power of God's Word bursts into human history as *the* truth — not just one more claimant to be the truth. The truth of revelation is the truth that saves. No matter how greatly it contradicts the wisdom of this world, the truth of revelation is *the* truth. The priest who participates in that divine action — that revelation — brings saving truth into the world of error, doubt, confusion, opinion, and conjecture.

In this sense the priest is a sign of the fullness of the revelation in Christ Jesus. What began as a revelation in the person of Jesus Christ is continued through the Church's priestly ministry, though it will be completed only as we enter into the presence of the Lamb enthroned. It is the role of the priest to proclaim with authority the revelation that contradicts the wisdom of this world and which brings believers to the kingdom of light in which we find life eternal.

To Govern. The second function of the priest is to lead or shepherd the faithful. Christ spoke with authority, but he also gave example. His life became iconic, an image of how a human life should be lived, how one person should treat another, how everyone should pray. So, today, our priests are also called to speak truthfully, to pray publicly and pray always, to guide souls in right morals, to correct and reprove the wayward, and to lead a life worthy of imitation.

To Sanctify. Jesus' life was also extraordinary insofar as he performed miracles that brought the power of God into the world. The Catholic priest shares even in those extraordinary moments: he brings divine power to the Church through the sacraments. Christ did not use his power to enhance his own position, but rather to lead the world to saving truth, so that truth itself could establish a community of believers. It is through those acts of divine power, the sacraments, that our priests today form the Church and sustain it and fill it with grace.

The priest celebrates the sacred mysteries. Traditionally, he has been called the "steward" or "dispenser of the mysteries of God." Whatever else the priest is, he is the earthly source of sacramental contact with Jesus. Jesus established the sacraments as the ordinary means of salvation. It is the priest who makes Christ the Savior sacramentally present.

By bringing human life into contact with the divine life, the priest does what's essential — what was willed by Christ himself — for the establishment of God's kingdom among us.

By the Sacrament of Holy Orders, a man is configured to Jesus Christ as Head and Shepherd of the Church. The change that takes place is irrevocable. It is permanent. The man is changed forever. He is a priest forever. Jesus' priestly identity is introduced into the life and being of the priest. Its purpose is to express the fact that Christ associated the Church with himself in an irrevocable way for the salvation of the world.

Nor is priesthood a temporary aspect of the kingdom. The Church's priesthood exists to reflect the permanent and transcendent union of Christ with his kingdom and to be a sign, a foreshadowing, of the final fulfillment of the kingdom. Jesus Christ is an eternal priest, always offering the perfect sacrifice of himself: "Christ . . . handed himself over for us as a sacrificial offering to God for a fragrant aroma" (Eph 5:2).

Now, *that* is the image of the perfect priest.

Thus, every priest testifies, with his very being, to the fullness of Christ's kingdom yet to come, but already begun in our midst.

———

Once I was with a retired priest when someone asked him to look back on more than seventy years of priesthood — a full lifetime of self-giving, self-emptying ministry. His response is one I will never forget. He said, "Somewhere, someplace a thousand years ago there was a priest; no one knows his name, no one remembers that he even existed. But because of his fidelity to his calling, centuries later I came to know Jesus Christ. Somewhere a thousand years from now, a young couple will bring their child to the baptismal font to receive the new life of Christ. It will be because of me!"

Hyperbole? Not really.

The priesthood is not just for today. Its graces go cascading down the millennia. It exists also to reflect the permanent and transcendent union of Christ with his kingdom. It is a sign today of the fullness of the kingdom.

CHAPTER 16

In the Court of the Kingdom

The Roman collar — the distinctive collar that priests wear — is a wonderful article of clothing. It's like a sign that says, "Go ahead. Ask me anything." It's an invitation for evangelization.

I was standing in line at the airport gate, waiting for my zone to board, when a man behind me — a young man, probably in his mid-thirties — decided to strike up a conversation.

"Could you explain something for me?"

I said I'd try.

He said that he'd been raised Catholic, "more or less," and he remembered that Catholics "do something that helps them get rid of all the excess baggage they carry around, so that they can start again brand new."

I said I assumed he was talking about the sacrament of confession.

"Yeah, something like that," he replied, and added that he just didn't "know how to use it."

No one had ever really told him the facts; nor had he ever had a chance to experience the "Catholic way of getting rid of excess baggage." All he carried with him was a vague

149

impression — which wasn't far from the mark — and perhaps an aching desire as well.

That young man is hardly unique. His experience of the confessional (or lack of experience) is replicated in hundreds of thousands of young adults across this land. That epidemic disconnect is at least part of the reason why we need a New Evangelization.

The young man at the airport wanted something, but didn't know where to go for it. He didn't know how to "do" that Catholic "something."

Those of us who *do* know about it should thank our parents, our pastors, and our catechists. Then we should pledge to tell a neighbor, a coworker, and a family member all about the way Christ, our heavenly king, dispenses mercy and justice in his kingdom.

———

All of us at times carry heavy "baggage" that we would like to unload. Despite our best intentions, each of us has experienced personal failure. The task of the priest is to help Catholics properly understand the power of the sacrament of confession to free us from the weight of our sins.

In Chapter 4 we discussed Jesus' healing of a paralyzed man, when the miraculous healing was itself merely a sign of the greater miracle: the forgiveness of sins. Years later, after his resurrection, Jesus appeared to his apostles and gave them the power to work that miracle. He breathed on them and said: "Receive the Holy Spirit. Whose sins you forgive are forgiven them and whose sins you retain are retained" (Jn 20:22-23). Thus he established the apostles and their successors as judges in his kingdom, with authority to dispense the abundant mercy of God. He said to his apostles: "Amen, I say to you that you who have followed me, in the new age, when the Son of Man is seated on his throne of glory, will yourselves sit on twelve thrones, judging the twelve tribes of Israel" (Mt 19:28).

Today, that office comes with priestly ordination, when the bishop prays over the newly ordained, asking that they be "worthy coworkers . . . so that your people may be renewed in the waters of rebirth and nourished from your altar; so that sinners may be reconciled and the sick raised up." From that moment on, the priest possesses a truly divine power: the ability to grant absolution for sins.

The Sacrament of Reconciliation is the story of God's love that never turns away from us. It endures our short-sightedness and selfishness. Like the father in the parable of the prodigal son, God waits, watches, and hopes for our return, every time we walk away. Like the son in the parable, all we need to do to return to our Father is to recognize our wrong, our need for forgiveness, and God's love.

———

Why do we need this sacrament? Well, why is it that we fail? Why is it so difficult at times to be good and to do what is right? Even though we may have good intentions, why do we often find ourselves doing what we know we should not do or failing to do the good we know we ought to do?

In the seventh chapter of his Letter to the Romans, St. Paul describes this situation while writing about what we call the human condition. "What I do, I do not understand. For I do not do what I want, but I do what I hate. . . . The willing is ready at hand, but doing the good is not. For I do not do the good I want, but I do the evil I do not want. Now if [I] do what I do not want, it is no longer I who do it, but sin that dwells in me" (Rom 7:15-20).

St. Paul's cry from the heart is something each of us has experienced. Why is it that we have the best of intentions, sincerely make New Year's resolutions, firmly renew our aspirations — sometimes every day — and then allow the worst in us to come out?

We can find an explanation in the opening chapters of the book of Genesis. A description of this seemingly relentless and endless struggle between good and evil is described in the imagery of the serpent tempting Adam and Eve with the forbidden fruit.

Adam and Eve ate the forbidden fruit. They chose their own desires over God's will and plan. This teaching, whatever the imagery, is very clear. Sin entered the world through the decision of a human being to choose self over God. God is not responsible for the evil in the world.

Each one of us is an heir to Adam and Eve. We are members of the human family. We trace our lineage back to this couple and their failure. The actions they took shattered God's created harmony not only for them, but also for us. Their sin is reflected in us and is mirrored in our daily life. This helps to explain why it is so difficult to do good, to do what we know we should do.

Yet we are not lost. God has not left us to our own devices. St. Paul, writing to the Corinthians, reminds us that just as in Adam sin was introduced into the world and, through sin, death and all of its consequences; so, too, grace and new creation come to us in Christ. Just as death came through a human being, so, too, the resurrection of the dead came through a human being. As in Adam all people die, so in Christ all shall be brought to life — a fullness of life in God's kingdom, a new creation already beginning in us through grace (see 1 Cor 15).

This is the message we proclaim when we face the mystery of sin, the reality of original sin, and the problems of the human condition that lead us to personal sin. Just as Adam brought sin, death, disharmony, confusion, disruption, and struggle into our lives, so too now Christ, the new Adam, gives us grace, redemption, new life, and salvation. It is in Jesus Christ that we now find the beginnings of the new creation. He leads us back to the Father, overcomes the tragic alienation of sin and restores harmony. Jesus gives us newness of life in grace that begins to restore our relationship with God which will lead to full communion with God in glory. It is for this reason that we identify Christ as the new Adam. Grace is the beginning of a new creation for all of those baptized into Christ.

Our struggle to renew the nation, our struggle to transform the culture, and our struggle to change the world, must begin with our own very personal response to God's gracious invitation to conversion.

When we face daily frustrations, we need to recall that we have the power to triumph over sin because we have Christ's grace within us. We have the capacity to be victorious, but we must renew the struggle every day with our Lord and Savior, the new Adam, Jesus Christ.

At the heart of the Sacrament of Reconciliation is God's mercy. The priest, as Christ's minister, listens to the confession to discover in the penitent's sorrow and openness to conversion, the grounds for forgiveness. He acts "in the person of Christ" as he hears the confession of guilt.

We acknowledge our guilt, but we do so with the full expectation of mercy, compassion, and, ultimately, absolution, because Christ has already atoned for our sins.

In a very graphic way the Stations of the Cross depict the power of sin, but also the power of grace to overcome sin. Jesus accepted the cross and took on our sins. Tradition tells us that he fell three times under the weight of the cross and got up

each time to continue his sorrowful way to Calvary, his cruci-
fixion, and our redemption — the way he would establish the
kingdom, once for all.

Each of us bears the weight of the crosses we fashion with
our own sins, and without God's grace we would never be able
to get back up after each fall.

In the creed we recite at Sunday Mass, we profess belief "in
the forgiveness of sins." Not only did Jesus die to wash away all
sin, and not only in his public life did he forgive sin, but after
his resurrection he also gave his Church the power to apply the
fruits of redemption — the authority to forgive sin.

This power to forgive sins is often referred to as the "power
of the keys." In the year 391, St. Augustine pointed out that
the Church "has received the keys of the kingdom of heaven so
that, in her, sins may be forgiven through Christ's blood and
the Holy Spirit's action. In this Church, the soul dead through
sin comes back to life in order to live with Christ, whose grace
has saved us."[41]

The *Catechism* tells us that the Sacrament of Reconciliation must be seen within the context of our conversion —
and God's kingdom. "Jesus calls to conversion. This call is an
essential part of the proclamation of the kingdom."[42] Even if
our conversion is ongoing and only partial, we still are subject
to the effort that will someday reach completion. St. Peter's
conversion, after he denied his Master three times, bears witness to Jesus' infinite mercy.

There can be no forgiveness if we do not have some regret,
if we do not have some measure of resolve not to repeat our
sin, if we do not intend to turn back to God. It is such sorrow
that leads us to the Sacrament of Penance. We may be impelled
by love for God or by fear of the consequences of our offense.
Whatever the motive, contrition is the beginning of forgiveness
of sin. The sinner must come to God by way of repentance.

True sorrow for sin implies a firm resolution not to fall back into it. It's true that we cannot be certain we will never sin again. Thus our present resolve must be honest and realistic. We must *want* to change, to be faithful to the Lord, and to take steps to make faithfulness possible. Christ's forgiveness always calls for such a commitment: "Go, [and] from now on do not sin any more" (Jn 8:11).

———

Many, many people would like to be rid of the baggage they're carrying. They'd like to "go" and never sin again. They're weary, and they need the strength that only God can give — the strength God wishes to give in the confessional.

In my archdiocese we launched a multi-year pastoral program to address this need. It's called "The Light Is On for You," and it's a simple invitation to confession. We put the word out via radio, a website, podcasts, Metro and bus advertisements, and roadside billboards. In every Catholic church across the archdiocese, every Wednesday night during Lent, the light would be on so that people would know there is a priest waiting for them.

Conversion experiences abounded. Not long after our launch, one veteran pastor told me that he had just heard a confession that, as far as he was concerned, made the whole program worthwhile. A younger priest added that, after hearing confessions one Wednesday for over three hours, he returned to his room and tearfully thanked God for this great priestly gift: the power to absolve sins, the grace to dispense the mercy of the divine king, and the privilege of extending the kingdom to one soul after another.

CHAPTER 17

Eucharist: Food for the Kingdom

Parishes traditionally mark Corpus Christi Sunday with a Eucharistic procession. The feast day's full name is the "Solemnity of the Body and Blood of Our Lord," so the sacred Host is often borne aloft and carried through the church — or even through the nearby streets — followed by a festive entourage of clergy and parishioners singing hymns.

It is one of those moments when we explicitly, publicly — and in a grand way — identify our Church with the kingdom. For the procession marks the advent of the great king. Our customs are adapted from the protocols observed by Old World towns when they received visits from their country's monarch. The people turned out to welcome the king. They dressed in their finest clothes and sang patriotic songs in his honor. We catch a glimpse of it in the Gospel's description of Jesus' triumphal entry into Jerusalem on Palm Sunday (see Jn 12:12-15).

What are we saying when we do this? *Here is our king! Jesus is truly present among us in this sacrament! Wherever he is, he reigns, and there is the kingdom!*

In my student days I once attended the famous procession at Genzano, a small Italian hill town south of Rome. In a custom that goes back to 1778, one of the principal streets of the community is covered with flower petals depicting artful designs and religious scenes. People work with great care and skill to cover the entire roadway, so that on the feast day the Sacrament can be carried from one church to another along an "avenue of flowers," a fitting carpet for the Eucharistic procession.

Corpus Christi processions take place in Catholic parishes all over the world (though few are as lavish as Genzano's). They are a sign of faith in the kingdom. They are an expression of faith in the presence of the king — his unique and abiding presence in the Eucharist.

Faithful to the Gospels, the Church teaches that Jesus is really present in the Eucharist — his body, blood, soul, and divinity — under the appearances of bread and wine. After multiplying a few loaves to feed a multitude of people, Jesus contrasted ordinary bread with the bread he would one day give, a bread that gives eternal life to those who eat it. He said: "I am the bread of life . . . I am the living bread that came down from heaven; whoever eats this bread will live forever; and the bread that I will give is my flesh for the life of the world" (Jn 6:48, 51). Confirming this promise as he fulfilled it, at his Last Supper he took bread and said, "This is my body." He took a cup of wine and said it was the chalice of his blood. Then he commanded his apostles, "Do this in memory of me."

So we do. Jesus promised us, "I will be with you always," and this is how he willed to be with us. This is why Catholics love the Mass. It's there we encounter the real presence of Jesus. It is a foretaste of the banquet that will be endless when the kingdom is fulfilled.

Jesus' real presence endures after the celebration of the Mass. That's why Catholic churches have a tabernacle. Once Communion has been distributed, the remaining Hosts are placed in the tabernacle to provide *viaticum* for those who are sick and home-bound. The tabernacle also provides a focal point for prayer and worship, since Christ abides there.

We express our Eucharistic faith in many ways: in genuflections, in prayer before the tabernacle, and in our regular attendance at Mass. Eucharistic piety is a distinguishing mark of a believing and practicing Catholic.

———

Thus I am dismayed when I read of studies that show that fewer than half of the Catholics in the United States regularly attend Mass. I am just as dismayed when I hear people say they look elsewhere on Sunday morning because they want to be a part of something that is more "lively" and engaging.

Can it be that so many people *just don't know* what's taking place in the Mass?

Yes, it's important to have good music. That's one way we should honor Jesus who is really present. But it is the divine presence that is essential to worship.

Similarly, the homily should be engaging and the people should feel welcomed, but these are not the reasons we go to Mass. The main reason is something that transcends each one of us — something objective that transcends me and my subjective preferences. At Mass we are invited into a mystery that carries us beyond our limitations and into the work of our redemption.

The Second Vatican Council put it memorably: "The liturgy is the summit towards which the activity of the Church is directed; at the same time it is the font from which all her power flows."[43] Elsewhere the council noted that the liturgy "is the primary and indispensable source from which the faithful are to derive the true Christian spirit."[44]

Liturgical prayer is more than community prayer. In establishing the Mass "in memory," Jesus was not asking for a historical commemoration, like the Fourth of July. He was commanding a re-presentation of his Paschal Mystery — his suffering, death, and resurrection — for the sake of every generation, in every place on earth. In the Mass we share in his life and passion, his rising and glory. We receive now what we hope we will possess in fullness in heaven.

Liturgy is the official public worship of the Church, the worship of the kingdom, as the king himself established it.

How sad the thought that so many baptized Catholics are staying away — sleeping in, enjoying a sports event, or otherwise walking away as Jesus asks, "Do you also want to leave?" (Jn 6:67).

We must improve our preaching, singing, welcoming, by all means. Our Eucharistic Lord deserves only the best of everything. But we must first improve our understanding. We must teach the Church's Eucharistic doctrine in a way that's clear and memorable — so that all these people can at least know what they're missing.

———

There are times, of course, when even a Catholic should not go forward for Holy Communion. But he or she should still attend Mass, and will certainly benefit from attending.

I recall one of the first weddings at which I officiated as a newly ordained priest. The time came for the distribution of Communion; and, after going to the bride and groom, I proceeded to the bridal party. One of the groomsmen caught my eye as I approached and almost imperceptibly shook his head "no."

I don't know the reason why he declined to receive Holy Communion. The reason was not my business. But to this day I have remained impressed with his personal integrity.

The Eucharist is indeed all that the Church says it is — all that Jesus said it would be. Therefore, we should acknowledge this fact by the way we receive — and, if necessary, by the way we defer. If we are conscious of having committed a mortal sin, we should hold back. If we have not been fulfilling the Church's norms for practicing the faith, we should hold back. Certainly non-Catholics should refrain from partaking of the Sacrament, because they do not share the Church's beliefs.

It is always good for us to be prepared for Holy Communion, and the best way to be prepared is by regularly going to the Sacrament of Reconciliation. St. Paul urges us to examine our conscience: "Therefore whoever eats the bread or drinks the cup of the Lord unworthily will have to answer for the body and blood of the Lord" (1 Cor 11:27). Before we approach the table of the Lord it is important to reflect on our life, ask God's forgiveness for our failings, and, if necessary due to serious sin, to avail ourselves of sacramental confession.

What do we bring to this Eucharistic banquet? We are guests who have been invited not just to *witness* the memorial of our redemption, but actually to *participate* in it. We are not just onlookers. By God's grace, we share in the work of redemption. So what do we bring? Certainly, we do not come empty-handed to the table of the Lord!

The first gift we bring is our own lively faith. Like Peter, we can reply when Jesus asks us, "Who do you say that I am?" that "You are the Christ, the Son of the living God." At Sunday Mass we do this repeatedly, and in great detail at the recitation of the creed. We profess our faith again when we go forward to receive the Eucharist. When the Host is presented with the declaration, "the Body of Christ," we mean it when we reply: "Amen," which means "I believe!" We mean it because we take it on the Lord's authority.

We also bring the gift of hope. Because we believe, because we see with the eyes of faith, because we place our trust in the words that Jesus has spoken to us, we can rejoice in the Mass, confident that this foretaste will be fulfilled in heaven, but also that the Sacrament will give us strength for living on earth. The Eucharist makes a difference in the way we look at the future, near and far. Receiving Holy Communion can provide us with a necessary attitude adjustment. As Pope Benedict XVI reminded us in his encyclical on Christian hope, "The one who has hope lives differently; the one who has hope has been granted the gift of new life."[45]

We should also approach the altar with hearts filled with love. The Eucharist unites us with Christ, and in Christ it unites us with one another. The Eucharist forms the Church and serves as its bond of love. What St. Paul preached, we sing in so many of our Communion hymns: we share one bread, and so we are one body.

The Church formed by the Mass is the enduring presence of God's kingdom in the world. Our "real presence" is utterly dependent on Jesus' real presence. Through the celebration of the Mass, the central event of salvation becomes truly present and the work of our redemption is accomplished. The Lord of history and Savior of the world is at work among us, just as he promised he would be.

CHAPTER 18

Manifesting the Kingdom

I like to imagine what Pope Benedict XVI saw, in April 2008, when he lifted his head after kissing the altar at Nationals Park in Washington, D.C. He looked out on a throng of almost fifty thousand people gathered for Holy Mass. The excitement was electric, the joy palpable.

He looked up and he saw the face of the Church in America, and it was undeniably Catholic — that is, *universal*, as Jesus intended his kingdom to be.

The face of America's Catholics is reflective of a multicultural heritage, from Africa, Central and South America, the Indian subcontinent, Asia, Australia, and Europe, as well as our own Native Americans.

Before the Holy Father was an image of our Church in all its richness. He beheld a living icon of the heavenly kingdom that unites every tribe and nation, every people, culture, and heritage — like the myriad saints and angels described in the Book of Revelation.

In his homily, the pope spoke to those people of their need to recognize the Church as the instrument of Christ's work today, mediating the action of the Spirit in the world. He told us, "Christ established his Church on the foundation of the

Apostles (see Rev 21:14) as a visible, structured community which is at the same time a spiritual communion, a mystical body enlivened by the Spirit's manifold gifts, and the sacraments of salvation for all of humanity. In every time and place the Church is called to grow in unity through constant conversion to Christ, whose saving work is proclaimed by Successors of the Apostles and celebrated in the sacraments. This unity, in turn, gives rise to an unceasing missionary outreach as the Spirit spurs believers to proclaim 'the great works of God' and to invite all people to enter the community of those saved by the blood of Christ and granted new life in his Spirit."

As that sacred liturgy unfolded, we heard the voice of the kingdom coming to be in our land. Music and song, hymnody and praise, woven into one great prayer emerging from hearts and voices made one in Christ. The crowd remained reverently silent as the opera diva Denyce Graves intoned, "We Are One, We Are One, We Are One in the Spirit." The truth that she sang, the Holy Father saw.

As we prepared to leave the ballpark after Mass that day, the Holy Father said to me, "That liturgy was a true prayer."

———

On the night before Jesus died, he prayed that all should be one, united to one another in the Church as Jesus himself was united to the Father: "so that they may all be one, as you, Father, are in me and I in you." He prayed that his disciples would be consecrated in truth, and he prayed that they would go forth into the nations as Jesus had gone forth from the Father: "As you sent me into the world, so I sent them into the world."

He sent his apostles forth to gather the world in worship. In our worship, especially at the Eucharist, we are a living manifestation of the kingdom coming to be.

The Mass is the preeminent breakthrough of the kingdom, but it is not the only one; and very few Masses take place with the kind of grandeur the Holy Father witnessed at Nationals Park.

Often we, like the Prophet Elijah discern the presence of God not in earthquakes and fire and mighty winds, but in the tiny whispering sound (see 1 Kgs 19:11-13).

Sometimes the light that points to Christ comes reflected through just one person. Sometimes the light that points to Christ will shine from some word you say, some gesture you make, your choice to be kind, your effort to smile when you would rather not.

———

When we turn toward Christ, we will reflect his light.

Before the invention of satellites or digital compasses and the Global Positioning System, travelers looked to the stars for guidance. A navigator would begin by locating the constellation called the Big Dipper, which in turn points to the North Star — the great light that mariners looked to as a guide.

To those who never made a journey, the sky perhaps appeared to be a jumble of flickering stars. But to be a mariner required skill and knowledge: the ability to name the stars and to see the heavens as something more than an undifferentiated scattering of lights.

The Gospel tells us about one particular star, a very significant star, and the task of this star. Its function was to point to the Lord Jesus. We read how it guided the Magi from the East — those "pagans" who represent the universality of the Church, the Church's inclusion of all peoples. Following the star, the Magi found their way to the otherwise inconspicuous place where baby Jesus lay.

What would have happened if there had been no star? How would the three Magi have recognized Christ? How would you and I have come to know that he is "God with us"?

Every year we celebrate the feast of the Magi, and we call it "Epiphany," which comes from the Greek word for "showing" or "manifestation." Without a showing, without a manifestation, Jesus could have gone through life without being recognized as God's Son — and, therefore, without accomplishing his goal. For Christ to have an effect in the world — in our neighborhoods, in our cities, in our lives — he has to be recognized. For Christ to be recognized, he has to be manifested.

One of the major difficulties today is the failure — collectively, societally, culturally, and socially — to recognize the place of God at the center of our lives. We face the same temptations as every generation before us. We have the same human nature and recognize the same challenges. Today, however, there is much less a sense of objective goodness and rightness in the world, because there is a much diminished recognition that Jesus is Lord, that Jesus is the source of goodness, light, and truth.

———

For two thousand years, it has been the work of the Church, all of us, every member of the Body of Christ, to show forth the presence of Jesus Christ, Savior and King, one of us who is also the Son of God. This showing takes place in many ways.

Just as there are countless stars in the sky that form all types of constellations, so, too, are there many, many holy lives, many kinds of dedicated people, women and men, disciples of Jesus, who replicate the work of the Great Star of Bethlehem. The Church continues to rely on that constellation of stars to manifest Jesus today and to lead people to him.

Who are the lights that manifest the kingdom of God for all to see? We have seen them repeatedly in the pages of this book. They are ordinary people who are doing the work of the kingdom in the places where they find themselves. They are parents speaking loving words to their children. They are children who give a positive example to their peers. They are attorneys defending the rights of others. They are craftsman and contractors who earn an honest living as Jesus did, building and fixing homes for better family life. They are doctors sharing the healing ministry of Christ. They are educators who teach as Jesus did. They are politicians who long to see the kingdom come with justice for their constituents. They are soldiers and farmers and fishers, as were so many of Jesus' first disciples. They make and sell clothing, like the early Christians we meet in the Acts of the Apostles.

Some directly serve the Church in its ministries. Perhaps they are on boards or committees. Perhaps we hear their voices proclaiming the word at Sunday Mass. Some of them take Holy Communion to the sick. Some are called to consecrated life or priesthood. They work in our cemeteries; keep the parish grounds; volunteer for festivals and altar societies, youth ministry, or PTA.

We could spend a day looking out and identifying light after light, star after star, in this great constellation that manifests the kingdom of God.

When the Magi found the Child Jesus, they presented gifts of gold, frankincense, and myrrh. Every person in the Church, each member of the heavenly constellation, has rich gifts to offer: your talents are yours, given by God, and the same is true of your time, your energy and, above all else, your love. These are yours to give, and only you can give them.

Just as Jesus came to be known in the homage and in the gifts that were given by the three Magi, so he becomes known, more clearly visible in the Church, because of your presence, your gifts, your witness.

———

The New Evangelization is all about the kingdom. The Epiphany star was directed to realizing the kingdom. So is the brightness reflected in the face of every believer today.

The New Evangelization is more an outlook on life than it is a program. It's an unceasing turning toward the Lord, returning to the Lord. It's about conversion — yours and mine, first of all — but also all the people we'll take along with us.

In every action, our starting point and goal must be Jesus Christ. Jesus calls this generation to follow him in discipleship and real friendship. But our response to his call can never remain simply a private or partial acknowledgment.

Yes, we'll see new programs arise in the Church, and that's all to the good. But God's plan always outdoes human projects. The New Evangelization is not a passing slogan. It is not a religious fad. It is not a transitory program, but a mystery that is as permanent as the earth, a glory eternal as the heavens.

As we accept Jesus' promise of life in abundance, we also lean upon his promise so that we might find strength in every situation, even those that stretch us and lead us to unfamiliar places.

Our personal commitment does not rest on our own individual resolve or limited resources. The First Letter of St. Peter reminds us: "You have been born anew, not from perishable but from imperishable seed, through the living and abiding word of God" (1 Pt 1:23).

Now is the opportune time. We can be confident that the Holy Spirit will enliven our commitment as we seek to rediscover the astonishing truths expressed in the creed. The Spirit will strengthen us as we entrust ourselves to the life of grace and virtue promised in the sacraments. The Spirit will bolster our confidence as we open our hearts for divine gifts that will strengthen us to live our faith. This must be our earnest prayer.

The call to *discipleship* involves *discipline*. We must welcome Jesus into our everyday lives, and we must do it every day. We should begin and end our days in prayer, read Scripture each day, or hear God's word and reflect on how to make it a part of our life. We should faithfully attend Mass and receive Our Lord in the Eucharist. We should actively accept his love and mercy in the Sacrament of Penance.

The New Evangelization can then overflow into the society in which we live. Together, as faithful parishioners and citizens, we are strong enough to adjust the cultural climate in our society so that the temperature is right for a substantial flourishing — the "new springtime" of which Pope John Paul II spoke. Grace builds on nature and cultivates culture. As we transform culture through our lives, we prepare a rich soil to receive the seeds of the Gospel, the seed of the kingdom.

The Sower entrusts this work to us. He already knows our difficulties and tensions, our restlessness, our faults and our human weakness. Nonetheless, he calls us and places the seed in our hands and entrusts it to our stewardship. The seed is the beginning of fruitfulness.

Planting the seed may mean that we learn new styles of communication; open our hearts to a more culturally diverse community; study more deeply the mysteries of the faith; reach out with confidence and invite a neighbor to attend Mass; forgive a long-held grudge; or focus on a new and more influential approach with a son or daughter, father or mother, or spouse who is away from the practice of the faith. Every moment becomes a new opportunity to connect another person with the abundant springtime that God promises. In this, we are protagonists of hope.

We are the agents of the New Evangelization. We are stars in the Church's constellation. We are the light set on the lampstand that manifests the coming of the kingdom.

CHAPTER 19

Till Kingdom Come

As the barbarian armies closed in on the great cities of Roman Africa, an old bishop watched from his residence. Some citizens, many of them his parishioners, were shoring up the walls against the inevitable onslaught. Others, meanwhile, despairing of help from God, turned to superstition. Still others abandoned themselves to the pleasures of the moment — looking out for Number One — as they held no hope for the future. All of them, including the bishop, were watching a world come to its end. It was the only world they had ever known. It was the imperial Roman world that had belonged to their parents and grandparents and many generations before them.

The elderly bishop was named Augustine, and he set himself the task of writing a book, a quite significant book, to make sense of what he saw — to make sense of the passing of one world, to lament the good things lost, and to fix his heart upon the things that would endure, even though Augustine's "world" should end.

Augustine was a patriot. He loved all that was good and noble in the culture of his *patria*, his native land. As a child and as a young man, he had committed to memory portions

of the epic poems and the great speeches of ancient Rome —
pre-Christian Rome. He never forgot those works, and he
quoted them freely in the great Christian synthesis he was
then composing, his *City of God*. He chronicled the deeds and
literature of the Romans, exhaustively, lovingly, but critically.
He called his fellow citizens to live up to all that was worthy in
their history and all that was beautiful in their culture, even as
it was vanishing, but still to embrace something better — the
revelation that could refine their heritage and save the souls of
their heirs, one by one.

Augustine believed that God's grace could build upon the
good he found in Roman culture. Grace could perfect them,
complete them, and fulfill them without destroying them. Perhaps the earthly empire could not be saved, but souls could be,
and they could learn how to live in any of history's successive
"worlds," for all of those worlds would fall as surely as they
rose. As Jesus reminded us, "Heaven and earth will pass away,
but my words will not pass away" (Mt 24:35). God's grace
could make something great even of the new world that was
only just beginning.

So he told the story of Rome, but he told it in the wid-
est possible context: the history of civilization. He showed
how, through all of history, there have been *two cities* upon the
earth: the City of God and the City of Man. You won't find
these cities on a map or on a globe. They are mystical cities.
Nor can you differentiate their citizens by the passports they
carry or by their ethnicity. You can tell their citizens by what
they love best: self over God (the City of Man) or God over
self (the City of God).

The City of God does not impose a temporal regime, and
it is compatible with any decent earthly government. Its citizens love the good in every society, in every culture, and they

reject only the things that are harmful to good and just earthly societies. Its citizens work for tranquil order in the lands they inhabit and for lasting peace on earth.

The City of God is not precisely synonymous with the Church — not yet anyway, though it will be in the fullness of time. For now, there are many non-Christians who are doing the work of God's city, even though they do not know it. And there are, sad to say, Christians who are not faithful to the city of their second birth. Until God's City comes to its perfection, our condition on earth will be mixed — the two cities will be mingled. To put it in terms of the parables: the wheat will grow among weeds, the net will teem with fish and trash, the treasure will be hidden in a vast and dusty field.

This is what Augustine saw as his world was ending, and he could not discern the shape of the world that would take its place.

Like Augustine, you and I live among a generation that has seen the passing of an old world and the rise of a new one, and many of us are at least ambivalent about the transition. For us as for Augustine, this is not simply an exercise in nostalgia. Augustine saw that many of the noble goods of Roman civilization would almost certainly vanish with the incursion of the barbarians. We, too, may wonder about the things that are passing away. We may question whether what has been described as the "greatest generation" is being succeeded by one of equal grandeur. We, too, may strive to discern, in the midst of all that seems so transient, the things that last.

Yet we also recognized that our sovereign God watches over history — the history of nations as well as our personal history — and is actively involved in its drama, its development. Jesus Christ is, moreover, working closely with those who live in his city, who labor for his kingdom.

As Jesus prepared to ascend into heaven, he turned over to his disciples a share in the mission entrusted to him by his Father. He gave them the power and the obligation to teach in his name. He said to them: "All power in heaven and on earth has been given to me. Go, therefore, and make disciples of all nations, baptizing them in the name of the Father, and of the Son, and of the Holy Spirit, teaching them to observe all that I have commanded you. And behold, I am with you always, until the end of the age" (Mt 28:18-20).

We are Jesus' disciples, and so we are there. We, too, have received the power and thus the obligation to share the Good News. Centuries may separate us from that initial group of followers, but *nothing* separates us from Christ, and it is he who issues the challenge. We are to be his witnesses. We must bear testimony to the truth, to the kingdom among us.

"You will be my witnesses." Those words launch the Acts of the Apostles (Acts 1:8). They launch the early Church. We must allow them to launch *our work* as we share the Good News, as we manifest and extend the kingdom of God.

In April 2008, Pope Benedict XVI came to the United States for the express purpose of encouraging us in our mission. He wished particularly to highlight the role of evangelization, catechesis, and education. As he began his homily at Nationals Park, he said, "In my exercise of my ministry as the successor of Peter, I have come to America to confirm you, my brothers and sisters, in the faith of the apostles [see Luke 22:32]. I have come to proclaim anew, as Peter proclaimed on the day of Pentecost, that Jesus Christ is Lord and Messiah." Throughout his visit, the pope both confirmed us in our faith and challenged us to share it and live it to the full.

That was his message. That was his prayer. We can be confident that God has answered his prayer.

Now our goal should be to take advantage of the Pentecostal outpouring of God's grace and love. Our mission is simple: to communicate the person and message of Christ. We are the heralds of the kingdom.

How do we proceed? How does it happen? All our lives are part of the Spirit's responding to the needs of today's generation. It is through our ordinary lives that the Church carries out her mission to proclaim and to manifest God's kingdom of grace, love, truth, justice, and peace.

We are always on the witness stand. Our lives tell others about the life of Jesus. We live and talk in such a manner that the truth of what we proclaim inspires them to accept and follow the Lord. We tell the story of Jesus with such conviction and with such power that others want what we have. Faith begins with this witness. The kingdom of God comes to be as the Word is proclaimed, embraced, and lived.

Authentic Catholic faith is never partial or selective. It is always universal. We say yes to the whole mystery of faith and to each of its elements, because we have placed our personal faith in God. We believe the truth of revelation because we believe God, and we believe that God is still teaching in and through the Church. When Peter came to recognize that Jesus was the Christ, the Son of the living God, he was prepared to believe any word of Christ, for it was clear to him that God is always to be believed. "You have the words of eternal life. We have come to believe and are convinced that you are the Holy One of God" (Jn 6:68-69).

The entire faith community must be invited into both the recognition that there is a need to evangelize and catechize and also the commitment to participate in this effort. This is perhaps the most challenging aspect of the New Evangelization — the announcement of the kingdom of God today. All of us together must assume responsibility for sharing with others the faith that we have received and so cherish.

We all need to learn to recognize the grace-filled opportunities that are ours. As the Holy Father said at Nationals Park, "the Church in the United States is now called to look to the future." Though he was confirming us, he said, in "the faith of the apostles," it was not a matter of ancient history. No, the Holy Father came "to proclaim anew, as Peter proclaimed on the day of Pentecost, that Jesus Christ is Lord and Messiah, risen from the dead, seated in glory at the right hand of the Father and established as judge of the living and the dead (cf. Acts 2:14ff)."

The pope spoke his word. Now, it's our turn. It's yours and mine.

This is surely a new Pentecost for the Church in our country. Our goal is to participate in that Pentecostal outpouring of God's grace and love by providing all with an understanding of the faith so that they are well equipped to live out their lives as witnesses to Christ, his Gospel, his kingdom.

We are witnesses. In the proclamation of the message of redemption, we have the words of everlasting life. We are a people alive in the Holy Spirit, and we must be motivated by our eagerness to share that extraordinary gift with the next generation.

Our task seems daunting, and it is! St. Paul taught us, though, how to find the strength to carry it through to completion: "I have the strength for everything through him who empowers me" (Phil 4:13). We find our strength in Christ and in his body, the Church.

Christ is still with us in his Church, really present in the Eucharist, alive in the gift of the Holy Spirit. The Church into which all Catholics have been baptized empowers us to stay connected to the Gospel, to the teaching of the Apostles, and to Christ.

We have been called to be apostles and empowered for the work of evangelization. Jesus beckons us. The joy we experience compels us to share it with others. We are not only disciples, we are evangelists. We cannot be one unless we are the other, too. Like those first disciples, we are called to envision ourselves walking alongside Jesus as the sower of the seeds of a new way of living, of a share in a kingdom that will last forever (see Mt 13:1-9, 18-23)

The Lord promises us that "the harvest is abundant." If the harvest is abundant, how much more so the seeds from which the harvest springs? Jesus frequently used the image of the seed to describe the hidden presence of his Word already among us.

We are — all of us — called to water, nurture, and cultivate those seeds already sown, or to plant new seeds where we recognize the opportunity. The ground may be rocky, filled with thorns, or heavily trafficked by many feet, but each and every Catholic can make a difference.

This is the New Evangelization.

———

Once while seated on a plane, I was approached by a flight attendant. She asked if I was a Catholic priest. (I was dressed, as usual, in clerical black.) I told her I was. She said she needed me to settle an argument the crew was having in the galley. Could I explain to her the Catholic doctrine on the "Second Coming of Christ"?

I told her, in a very summary way, what I have tried to say in the course of this book: that the kingdom has come with Jesus Christ, that it is growing gradually and imperceptibly, and that it will achieve its fullness only with God's decisive intervention at the culmination of history. Christ will return to claim his kingdom.

"Ha!" she said. "I was right!"

Catholics can sometimes feel inadequate when their non-Catholic friends cite Bible verses at them. But I've found that Catholics really do know the Bible as well as others. They know the parables by name — though they're not in the habit of citing a verse for them. They know the Psalms because they've sung all the responsorials at Mass. They know the stories — the woman at the well, the Passion, the resurrection — because they've heard them proclaimed on countless Sundays. They know how the grand story ends: with the coming of the kingdom in power, in glory, in its fullness.

Catholics today look for a kingdom, just as they did in the time of St. Justin Martyr (whom we quoted in Chapter 1) in the mid-second century. We look for a kingdom in our day-to-day lives. We look to the kingdom in its plenitude, as Christ has promised it will come, if we pray to the Father: "Thy kingdom come!"

It makes all the difference in the world if we know what we're praying for.

———

In his first homily as Chief Shepherd of the Universal Church, Pope John Paul II offered words that were at once consoling and challenging. They soon became a byword for the whole Church. He called us "to open wide your hearts to Christ." He pleaded with us: "Do not be afraid, open your hearts to Christ."

Twenty-three years later as he concluded the celebration of the great millennium, the Jubilee Year 2000, he called upon all of us once again, and this time he issued the challenge that Jesus issued so long ago to a boat full of weary fishermen. Blessed John Paul told us to "set out into the deep" — in Latin, *duc in altum*.

We can do that. We can fearlessly put out into the deep. We can proclaim the message of Christ and work to realize his kingdom among us. This the Church has always done with confidence and assurance. For we know that, even in the face of difficulty, we can joyfully, confidently, and lovingly share the words that give life. The Spirit speaks in us, and the Spirit gives us words (see Lk 12:12).

We pray, "Thy kingdom come" with anticipation, aware of so much more that is yet to be ours. God's kingdom is our goal, our vision, and our prayer.

Thanks to Christ and thanks to his Church, you and I have heard the words: "The kingdom of God is at hand." Let us never hold back, and let us always rejoice to share those words, to manifest the kingdom in our lives, and thus proclaim the good news of Christ. We have heard and accepted the call: "You will be my witnesses."

Through all of us, others come to hear, embrace, and love the message:

> Christ has died.
>> Christ is risen.
>>> Christ will come again!

Afterword

Robert P. George

Betrayed by his friend, arrested by the authorities, and brought before the Roman governor, Jesus was asked point-blank by Pontius Pilate: "Are you a king?" "My kingdom," he replied, "is not of this world."

Was this merely a clever answer by a quick wit who found himself in a tough spot?

Apart from the light of faith, we might suppose so. Jesus *was*, after all, in a tough spot. And his answer to Pilate's question almost got him out of it.

Only days earlier, Jesus had been welcomed into Jerusalem, the provincial capital, by a palm-branch-waving throng who proclaimed him the successor to his ancestor, King David, who many hoped and believed would restore the sovereignty and authority of Israel. To have admitted that he was, or aspired to be, a king — at least in any ordinary sense of the word — would have been to forfeit his life. Roman governors came in better and worse varieties, but none was soft or sentimental; none would show tolerance for, or mercy toward, anyone who set himself up as a rival to Roman authority.

Yet evidently Pilate was satisfied with Jesus' answer. It persuaded him that, whatever Jesus was — a dreamer, perhaps, or a crank, some sort of holy fool — he posed no threat to Rome. Had the crowd baying for Jesus' blood let Pilate get away with it, the governor would have been content to give Jesus a few lashes and send him on his way. Of course, in the end, the mob got what it wanted, warning Pilate that refusal to execute a claimant to kingship would make him "no friend of Caesar." No Roman governor who cared about his career — or his life — could afford that. So, in the end, Pilate sent Jesus to be crucified and (following the Roman custom of giving public notice of the charge against a capital criminal) ordered a sign to be posted above his head: "Jesus of Nazareth, King of the Jews."

But let us return to Pilate's question and Jesus' reply. Viewed in the light of Christian faith, Jesus' answer is anything but a desperate man's brilliant (if finally unsuccessful) attempt at escaping death. It is, rather, *a revelation of who Jesus is.* Yes, Jesus was — and is — indeed a king, but not in any ordinary sense. He did not seek to displace the Roman emperor or even the puppet ruler of Judea, King Herod, as a political sovereign. He did not pose *that* kind of threat to worldly powers. The rule he claimed — and claims — is rule over the human heart. What he demands is not tribute, in the manner of earthly kings, but repentance and reform. What he seeks is not outward conformity, something ordinary rulers, good or bad, can be satisfied with, but a change *within* us — the transformation of hearts and minds that Christians call *conversion.*

In the fallen human condition, the temptation we all experience is to live for self-satisfaction — to seek the gratification of one's desires, whatever they happen to be. But King Jesus wants us to live differently. He wishes to come into our hearts so that by grace through faith we can conquer our greatest enemy — selfishness — and live for what is good and right and true and loving and holy. Jesus' message is not "if it feels good, do it," or "I'm OK, you're OK"; it is "seek ye first the kingdom," which means "take up your cross and follow me," and "go, sell what you have and give to the poor, then come and follow me." For the sake of the kingdom, Jesus asks us to be prepared to sacrifice every worldly thing we might treasure — wealth, power, status, prestige, comfort, pleasure, the good opinion of others.

It is clear then that the demands of this king — the King of kings — go far beyond the commands of earthly potentates. He requires far greater and more difficult sacrifices. Indeed, humanly speaking, Jesus' demands are impossible to meet. (Consider, for example, his strict injunction that we love — *love*, mind you — not only our friends and those who mean us no harm, but even our enemies.) Apart from divine grace, no one could possibly live up to what Jesus calls us to do. Yet, through him, with him, and in him, those of us who are his followers believe we are given the grace to do it. Jesus himself said: "Nothing is impossible with God."

To be sure, we Christians sometimes — alas, one must say often — stumble and fall; we slip into our old ways and bad habits; we yield to selfishness and fail in Christ-like, self-sacrificial love. Even St. Peter, the leader of the apostles, the one who declared Jesus to be "the Christ, the son of the living God," denied him three times. As sinners, we ourselves deny him by our deeds, even if we are faithful to him in words. Yet Jesus forgave Peter and forgives us. Indeed, no matter how abjectly or how often we fail, Jesus is always there to pick us up, dust us off, and encourage us in the lifelong, never-ending process of conversion — a process that begins with baptism and ends only with death.

Is the effort worth it? Absolutely. While earthly rulers have sought domination, King Jesus offers liberation — liberation from the most abject and dehumanizing forms of servitude, from subjection to one's own base wants and brute desires; from slavery to self, bondage to sin.

To preach the Gospel of Jesus Christ is to preach the kingdom Our Lord proclaimed — a kingdom of true freedom and dignity; a kingdom, in words quoted by the fathers of the Second Vatican Council, "of truth and life, of holiness and grace, of justice, love, and peace"; a kingdom that is, as the Council taught, already present in mystery here on earth, yet still to come in full flower when the Lord returns in glory.

In the chapters of this book we are taught about this kingdom that is unlike any other by a master preacher and catechist, Cardinal Donald Wuerl of the Archdiocese of Washington. Cardinal Wuerl has devoted his priestly ministry, and the whole of his life, to understanding as deeply as possible the profound beauty and mystery of Christ's kingdom, and communicating this understanding to his fellow Catholics and all men and women who wish to know who Jesus is and what he offers to hearers of his word.

In a sense, the cardinal offers nothing novel in these pages. His message is Christ's message. It is the message transmitted to us by the apostles who walked with Jesus and talked with him, shared his ministry and, after his death, resurrection, and ascension, were inspired and empowered by the Holy Spirit — promised and sent by Jesus himself — to "go and make disciples of all nations." It is the message of the Church, founded by Christ on Peter, "the rock," who, having repented of his cowardly denials of Jesus, took the Savior's message — of love and healing, true joy and authentic freedom — to Rome, and in that center of worldly power gave his own life in martyrdom for Christ's kingdom.

Bishops are successors of the apostles. Their mission is to bring us to an encounter with Jesus, our living Lord, and to teach us to walk in his ways. In the institution of the Church, they are, to be sure, administrators — executives, we might say today — but even here their task and responsibility go far beyond efficiently running dioceses and overseeing the work of Catholic parishes, schools, hospitals, and the like. Yes, governing is an element of the threefold ministry of a bishop (a ministry, as Cardinal Wuerl reminds us, that is shared in by priests); but so are teaching and sanctifying. In the book you hold in your hands, Cardinal Wuerl teaches us so that we might be sanctified. He leads us in the way of holiness. The whole point of his labors is to bring us to the encounter with Jesus that makes conversion possible. Our task as readers is simply to be open to that encounter.

Princeton, New Jersey
September 2011

Acknowledgments

Anyone acquainted with my television program "The Teaching of Christ" will recognize some of the examples in this book and even the general theme of the kingdom of God as it is manifested in our world. For seventeen years, "The Teaching of Christ," a half-hour television program on the Catholic faith, aired each Sunday on CBS's Pittsburgh affiliate, KDKA TV, and later during the week on cable networks across our country.

When the publisher of Our Sunday Visitor first proposed that I write a book about the kingdom, I demurred on the grounds that I wouldn't have the time. After all, I do have a day job.

However, I was persuaded when reminded of my old television show and the constancy with which I returned to the theme of the kingdom.

So I went back to my colleagues from the show, and asked if they could help me gather the transcripts. They kindly agreed, and before long I found ample material for a book — or three, or four . . .

I thank Father Kris Stubna and Jeff Hirst for their generous assistance during that research phase. I thank Nancy Lippert and Father Ronald Lengwin for their help, all those years ago, as I prepared and taped "The Teaching of Christ."

I greatly appreciate Mike Aquilina, who so carefully went through this work with the skill of a master editor.

I am grateful to Greg Erlandson and Cynthia Cavnar of Our Sunday Visitor for their encouragement. My hope is that readers might find the reading of the book as satisfying as I found the writing of it.

There is so much more to say about the mystery of the kingdom — a mystery more vast than the world, more varied than everything in creation. If anyone should say that this, that, or another point could have been included, I'll probably agree. And I'll offer the inspired excuse of a long-ago author: "There are also many other things that Jesus did, but if these were to be described individually, I do not think the whole world would contain the books that would be written" (Jn 21:25).

Notes

1. St. Justin Martyr, *First Apology* 11.
2. Pope Benedict XVI, *Jesus of Nazareth: From the Baptism in the Jordan to the Transfiguration* (New York: Doubleday, 2007), 47.
3. *Catechism of the Catholic Church*, n. 567.
4. *Catechism of the Catholic Church*, n. 865.
5. *Catechism of the Catholic Church*, n. 1060.
6. *Catechism of the Catholic Church*, n. 680.
7. *Catechism of the Catholic Church*, n. 1107.
8. Origen, *On First Things* 1.3.
9. St. Augustine of Hippo, *City of God* 20.9.1.
10. St. Augustine of Hippo, Sermon 125.
11. St. Augustine of Hippo, Sermon 223.
12. St. John Chrysostom, *Homilies on Matthew* 43.7.
13. St. John Chrysostom, *Homilies on Romans* 23.
14. *Catechism of the Catholic Church*, n. 1025, italics added.
15. *Catechism of the Catholic Church*, n. 786.
16. *Catechism of the Catholic Church*, n. 898.
17. *Catechism of the Catholic Church*, n. 2832.
18. See Pope John Paul II, Post-Synodal Apostolic Exhortation *Christifideles Laici* (1988), n. 15.
19. Second Vatican Council, Dogmatic Constitution on the Church, *Lumen Gentium*, n. 31.

20. Pope John Paul II, "Jesus' Earthly Life Is a Model for the Laity," General Audience, November 10, 1993.

21. *Catechism of the Catholic Church*, n. 2478.

22. *Catechism of the Catholic Church*, n. 680.

23. *Catechism of the Catholic Church*, n. 677.

24. St. Clement of Rome, *Letter to the Corinthians* 44.1-2.

25. *Catechism of the Catholic Church*, n. 874.

26. *Catechism of the Catholic Church*, n. 882.

27. *Catechism of the Catholic Church*, n. 886.

28. *United States Catholic Catechism for Adults*, chapter 3.

29. *Catechism of the Catholic Church*, n. 889.

30. *Catechism of the Catholic Church*, n. 894.

31. *Catechism of the Catholic Church*, n. 893, citing *Lumen Gentium* 26.

32. This principle has been enshrined, since 1983, in the Church's law; and Catholic priests are "not to have an active role in political parties..." (c. 287, 2).

33. Second Vatican Council, *Apostolicam Actuositatem*, 16.

34. Pope John Paul II, *Christifideles Laici* (1988), n. 3.2.

35. *Ibid.*, n. 3.6.

36. Congregation for the Doctrine of the Faith, *Doctrinal Note on Some Questions Regarding the Participation of Catholics in Political Life* (January 16, 2003).

37. Pope John Paul II, Encyclical Letter *Evangelium Vitae*, n. 28.

38. Pope Benedict XVI, Encyclical Letter *Deus Caritas Est*, n. 29.

39. See *Catechism of the Catholic Church*, n. 2223.

40. *Catechism of the Catholic Church*, n. 1783.

41. St. Augustine of Hippo, Sermon 214.

42. *Catechism of the Catholic Church*, n. 1427.

43. Second Vatican Council, *Sacrosanctum Concilium*, 10.

44. *Ibid.*, 14.

45. Pope Benedict XVI, Encyclical Letter *Spe Salvi*, n. 2.